# NORMAL
# KINGDOM BUSINESS

Also by *WORLD Magazine*:

Salt, Not Sugar
Won't Let You Go Unless You Bless Me

# NORMAL KINGDOM BUSINESS

*A collection of essays*

BY
Andrée Seu

Reprinted edition originally published November 2006
*WORLD Magazine* edition, May 2006

Essays in this book were first printed, in one form or another,
as columns in *WORLD Magazine*, for which Andrée Seu is a senior
writer. Some essays have been revised for this book while
others remain as they were originally printed in Andrée Seu's
*WORLD Magazine* column.

Book design and text composition by Matthew Mulder
Set in Xavier Dupré's Reminga
Cover illustration by Krieg Barrie


Printed in the United States of America
10 9 8 7 6 5 4 3 2 1

ISBN-13: 978-0-9779299-6-2
ISBN-10: 0-9779299-6-5

for Babe and Paulette Mailloux, parenting me beyond
the statute of limitations

# CONTENTS

Andrée Seu

# INTRODUCTION

*From an e-mail exchange on December 21, 2005:*

ANDRÉE: Say, what do you think Jesus did for fun? Or was his only pursuit of joy that of doing the Father's work (John 4:34)?

RONNIE: I'll bet he liked to run and was fast. He probably had a way of making you laugh and cry simultaneously. Fishing was boring for him because he caught one each time he threw his line in the water, since fish are not plagued with unbelief. When he baked unleavened bread, the loaf wanted to rise in tribute, yeast or no. I guess he learned to use "Peace, be still" in order to get some sleep, as all of creation was cacophonous in its symphony of praise to him. Above all, I think he is a cool and ultimately groovy guy and I look forward to us hanging out for the next few eternities, hey?

—Andrée Seu
—Ronnie Rudd

# NORMAL KINGDOM BUSINESS

*A collection of essays*

# JE ME SOUVIENS

*I remember, and He will remember*

*JE ME SOUVIENS.* TO you it's the slogan on a license plate from that other world across the border. To me it's tourtierre for Christmas breakfast, galettes at a summer cookout, and singing "Ô Canada" to a maple leaf flag in school just after "The Star-Spangled Banner."

Not that I was born in Quebec but more like a stage reproduction of it, a *trompe l'oeil* of culture, with Ste. Anne de Beaupre in miniature on the banks of the Blackstone.

We're talking about a hemorrhaging of humanity southward from the St. Lawrence River around 1900, pooling in little pockets of a territory that, evidently, it was not France's "manifest destiny" to possess: Manchester, Nashua, Concord, Claremont (New Hampshire); Lewiston, Waterville, Biddeford, Sanford (Maine); Fall River, New Bedford, Central Falls (Massachusetts); Woonsocket, Rhode Island.

Disaffected farmers they were, these less glorious

sons of Jacques Cartier and Samuel de Champlain, men weary of nine months of snow-bitten earth (the natives say there are two seasons in Quebec: winter and construction) and lured to that new invention of Samuel Slater's, the textile mill, with its promise of a slight easing of the curse of Adam.

Besides cheap labor, they imported their language to New England. There it languished, and there it died, in that graveyard of all languages, America. It was a deed that took four generations and was complete by mine. Still, we might all be speaking French today if Francis I had not been an indifferent patron of exploration, and Henri IV had not been busy waffling on his Catholic or Protestant identity.

It was back to this land that my friend Lynn decided I should go and that she should take me. And so, not at all sure that I could go forward, I journeyed backward in the summer of '99.

And it was Europe again!—the smells and window boxes and narrow winding cobblestone roads like the crooked lines of a preschooler's drawing. And it was breakfast in sun-drenched sidewalk cafés by tree-lined streets hosed nightly and still shimmering, the way Monet does shimmering. And we rode the *caleche* through the Plains of Abraham and conjured the ghosts of Generals Wolfe and Montcalm in that fateful battle of 1763. And it was stick bread carried under the arm and shared with cheese and *mille feuille* on our terrace overlooking the Ursuline convent gardens. And we guessed about Madame Chouinard and Monsieur Giroux who ran the inn. And yes, we even laughed, and for six days pretended that life was only beautiful.

And all those childhood names I knew—Légaré, Desjardin, Godbout, Lefèbvre—I saw lacquered on the sides of tourist buses, on street signs, on banks, the lithographs of local artists, like some surrealistic reconfiguration of my past, a *déjà vu*. And, wondering who I was now that I was not a wife, I went, alone on Saturday, to Lavale University and pored over yellowing marriage records and pushed back the darkness a few generations—Mailloux, Perrier, St. Pierre, Lambert, Laflame, Belhumeur, Fontaine, Champagne. But it didn't feel like family.

On Sunday, on the Rue St. Louis we found a church of fellow transients where we all sang common hymns and remembered a common Father and a common emancipation. And it felt like family. A better genealogy.

*Je me souviens:* "I remember." The homage we give our fathers. What the Recabites were commended for, and the Israelites stumbled over. And now one greater than Cartier and Montcalm is here, one more worthy of our cultivating a remembrance.

I had been feasted sumptuously. I wanted to pay—a croissant, a taxi fare, something. But Lynn explained that it was a gift. And I could see the truth in it. And how it is that we like to pay our own way, not because we are so good but because we are so evil. Never mind, she will be repaid on the day the books are opened (Revelation 20:12). *Moi, je me souviens. . . . Et le Seigneur aussi, il se souviendra.*

# ON WRITING

---

*Know the rules, and how to break them the right way*

THE BIGGEST HELP TO my writing has been the discipline of having to fit everything into 800 words. That's on the craft side. On the inspiration side it's the daily reading of Scripture. The World Journalism Institute gave me three hours to tell students in Asheville how I write, but I had only those two points, really. WJI could have saved a little money.

I read a whole book on potty training once. A yellow highlighter boiled the essentials down to an ounce of meat sandwiched between airy bread. What follows is my ounce of meat.

How to write an essay: You're drifting off and a thought pops in, and it sounds like a lead sentence so you jot it on the pad you keep under the bed. You look for sleep, but an idea tugs at your ear, till you finally give in and brainstorm it for all it's worth, the gems and junk alike. Come daylight, you mentally solve syntactical problems while molding meatballs.

Then you sit in front of a white page, terrified. You phone your mother crying, "This is ridiculous! Who am I kidding, I can't write!" Which is all well and good, but eventually you have to face the paper. You take a deep breath and say, "OK, don't make art, just make sense."

Good writing is confident and lean. Compare the first sentence of this piece with an alternative: "There are perhaps many helpful tips for writing, but in my opinion, one of the most helpful may be to try to fit everything you have to say into an essay of approximately 800 words." Zzzzzzzzzzzz. The reader has already gone to the kitchen to make "s'mores."

Replace generalities with vivid details. "Gone to the kitchen to make "s'mores" is slightly better than "gone to the kitchen for a snack"—which is better than an abstraction about the reader's "waning interest." "Brief fame": forgettable; "15 minutes of fame": a keeper. And if Abe Lincoln had said "Many years ago" instead of "Four score and seven years ago," he'd have been right that the world would "little note nor long remember."

Conversational writing doesn't mean indifference to grammar; learn the difference between a comma and a semi-colon. On the other hand, forget what Sister Clair said in third grade about always needing a subject and a verb. Not so. But know how to break the rules the right way.

Thou shalt avoid clichés. Thou shalt not hold out for the perfect lead—a good lead will do. Thou shalt not try to produce the definitive article on democracy; a helpful one will do (Acts 20:20).

Jesus told stories. Think about it.

Say things in a starling way ("If your eye causes you to sin, pluck it out.") Then be ready to take your lumps in the "letters to the editor."

Dr. John Frame told me this: Let the fruit of the spirit be your guide. Think about how love, joy, peace, patience, gentleness, goodness, faithfulness, kindness, and self-control can inform your writing.

Don't freak out at a lousy first draft; no one sees it but you and God. Read and reread your drafts. Read them aloud, checking for rhythm. Shoot for clarity, and style will be its handmaiden. Make every word carry freight. (That doesn't mean every word must be "informational"; you may sometimes sacrifice content for color.)

Be ruthless: "Kill the little darlings"—the ideas off point, the favorite insights and flourishes that are just to show off. Simplify where possible. Nuke the adverbs. At a certain stage in the process, writing is just a mathematical problem: matters of logic, redundancy, coherence, transitions, word-counting.

Dirty little secrets of the trade: (1) Writers don't know where they're going till they get there; (2) There's no such thing as an original thought.

Your first exercise: Write a thousand-word essay, as tight as you can make it. Then slash it by 50%.

Find the nearest exit and get out.

# FOSSILIZED REMAINS

———————————•———————————

*What our greeting cards will say about our culture*

LESSON ON POSTMODERNISM: SKIP the books, go straight to the greeting-card aisle of your local apothecary. When space aliens unearth 21st-century civilization in ages hence, fossilized remains of "American Greetings" and "Hallmark" specimens will tell all. Here is the repository of all men's hopes, desires, and fears—in philosophical fast-food form. Here, the heart of the matter reduced to the grinding labor of minimum-wage poets, or the humor of *Seinfeld* writer wannabes, ribald little jokes worth a thousand doctoral theses.

It started as a Christmas expedition. I was after gifts, not cards; but the little bristol board art works were everywhere, and I was drawn in by the hordes who paused for long silences, like priests with heads bowed, before the altars of myriad-colored messages in endless rows.

The harried greeting-card pilgrim, in his quest for

just the right personal message from an impersonal message factory, is helped by the thoughtful corralling of cards into their logical niches ("niche" being a key concept in postmodernism, where many "stories" exist side by side, all true on their own terms and none truer than its neighbor).

The sweet innocence of the child's Mother's Day appreciation is in its own place, the bawdy adult perspective on life's various milestones in another. (It is assumed by card makers that innocent children will grow up to be bawdy adults, though precisely where this transformation takes place is not clear from a casual perusal of the racks of cards; alien archaeologists will have to spackle gaps in the fossil record with creative theories on this point. This may prove challenging if they have no concept of sin.)

The humble card rack will be a rich vein of information on the rites of passage of the mortal biped. Among the occasions celebrated are births and deaths, weddings and engagements, lost teeth and job promotions, and every sacrament of the Roman Catholic Church except Extreme Unction. Moreover, you can have your religious observances to include God or not, as you prefer. ("Preference" is another important idea for postmodernist.)

"Age Jokes" begin at "30" and run for 10-year

increments till "60," where they fall eerily silent. These tiresome jabs at declining physical functions are not so much Dylan Thomas's "rage against the dying of the light" as sheer denial. When in the adjacent section we meet the somber "Sympathy" card, it is as if death has come by surprise. (These hermetically sealed compartments are a postmodern hallmark.) To their credit, I suppose, these "Sympathy" sentiments do not seek to soothe by leaps of prognostication as to the eternal destiny of the "beloved departed," but focus on the bereaved himself, emoting vague wishes of "peace" and "comfort."

A category for "loss of pet" will be found near "loss of father" (postmodern enlightenment has evolved to a realization that animals are equal in value to people —after all, both kinds of creatures have mouths and chromosomes and oxygen requirements).

There is trouble in Hallmark paradise, however, as the Martian explorer will soon surmise by the section devoted to "troubled relationships" and to saying "sorry." Equally disturbing are the increasingly common and slightly awkward concessions to "blended" families: birthday cards to Mom & Stepfather, Dad & His Wife, etc. Postmoderns join and split almost casually, having no Absolute glue to hold the center: A card whose front portrays a woman in jail-bird stripes, kicking off a ball and chain, bears the text, "Free at Last"—and then inside, the felicitation, "Congratulations on your divorce."

Time does not permit to speak of Kwanzaa salutations, hair-stylist and dog-sitter thank-yous, good-luck wishes, and a dozen ways to showcase the "Serenity Prayer" (the perfect nonreligious religious card for people who have lost God but still have a God-sized hole in their souls). Nor have we leisure to analyze the whole line of male-bashing cards that women delight to send to other women. (Interestingly, no female-bashing cards are to be found for the guys. Deprecation of the female is available, mainly in monotonously recycled snide remarks about women's failing body parts, but these are strictly for women from women.)

The overall impression for the hitchhiker through the galaxy will be gleaned, however, from no individual card so much as from taking in the rack at a glance. He will marvel at a time in human history when, having lost sight of the Truth, the creature was left, in its void, with endless, soulless Choice.

# DEATH BY DETAIL

—————•—————

*The pitfalls of being too busy*

I'M REALLY TOO BUSY to write this essay. I've been slighting people all day long, perfecting minimalist, utilitarian exchanges till it's almost an art form. The newspaper makes an arc from the front porch to the back recycling bin with nary a skid across the kitchen table. My youngest child told me she doesn't remember what a family dinner is, and the house has gotten licks and promises the past three years.

You're too busy to read this too, I know—which is why it's nice to have this one-page, 750-word format with a drawing in the middle. A bite size you can wolf down over your half cup of coffee.

I don't know how we arrived at this place. It's all part of the "unintended consequences" of scientific advances in convenience, I guess, like the way electronic mail just gives you one more thing to check every day.

A Minnesotan missionary to Turkey thanked me

once for not saying, in my letters, how "busy" I am, like everybody else in the States does (A close shave! I was just about to mention that to her!). "What is everyone so busy doing?" she wrote, with gentle reproach, and then proceeded to expand on the importance and joy of lingering over humble meals with her Kurdish neighbors, something with which I am principally in total agreement.

I've asked the Lord to make me smarter, or diminish my need for sleep, so that I can be more efficient, but I'm not sure He works that way. He'll probably say, "My grace is sufficient for you, My power made perfect in weakness." As it is, the present situation curtails my independence and keeps me nagging God for help all day long—which I suppose is the whole idea.

A friend grabbed me at the seminary café and shared amazing news. Something inside had told her to phone her brother last week. "If you hadn't called, I was going to commit suicide the next day," he said. It wasn't idle talk; he had the method, the time, the place, the note, all planned. She dropped everything and met him—and took an "F" on her Hebrew exam. The story gave me pause.

But just for a moment. Then it was off to Restaurant Depot after hours for supply buying, as my helper had just resigned (she was too busy), and then to see about the van's pull to the left, the diseased tree in the backyard, a leaky hot water tank, laundry and dinner before "Pioneer Girls" at 7, a desk that resembles a Middle Eastern tell with just the top layer excavated, and my son's sixth-grade teacher who wants a conference ASAP. Death by detail.

I heard that John Wesley or Martin Luther or somebody (I don't have time to track down the reference) prayed three hours daily—except when he had a busy day ahead, and then he prayed six hours. I hope that's apocryphal.

A pitfall of being busy is that one tends to look down on others who "waste" time in idle pursuits— such as having conversations, going out to dinner, or coloring unicorns with 8-year-olds. Perhaps a self-study on the Martha and Mary story of Luke 10:38-42 is in order. When I have time.

I remember the day, in mid-marriage implosion, when Donna B. stood with me in the church parking lot till the shadows shifted across the pavement. I don't know what list of chores she mentally "X"ed off as I emotionally purged, nor what her family had for dinner that night, but I drove away filled. Tough call, Donna. Thanks.

I sense there is something wrong with a day whose success is predicated on an allowance of 30 seconds per conversation. Jesus brooked interruptions

(Matthew 14:13-14). I am groping toward some solutions: such as, henceforth, not to let the "perfect" be the enemy of the "good" (the friend I cannot invite for dinner I will at least phone), and to meditate more on the parable of the Good Samaritan. Moreover, a nebulous insight is taking shape: that there is really only one priority in life—the glory of God—and under that its several distributions, and necessary trade-offs, to sort out "with fear and trembling." Any help in fleshing this out will be greatly appreciated; just contact my e-mail. I've gotta run.

# THE DIRT ON DIRT

*It's common, abundant—and a glorious gift from God*

THE YEAR I WAS in landscaping after my husband's death, a friend gave me a book titled *Dirt*, which landed on the shelf and has sat there since, collecting dirt. Why should I read a paean to compost rather than David McCullough's *John Adams*? But almost as a dare the gift has been dusted off now, a gauntlet thrown at the author's feet: Go ahead, make dirt interesting for 200 pages.

I have long had such an adversarial relationship with soil (shoes are left at the door in my house, in Korean style—the one house rule I've dug in my heels on) that I had forgotten the love affair I once had with the stuff.

It was 1975 and I was saved, and the world was new and all, and Sally and I took old Mrs. Chesbrow's half acre and turned it into a garden to make Nebuchadnezzar proud. It wasn't our doing, of course, and that was the wonder of it. We gave the earth seed and it gave us back zinnias, and bachelor buttons, and snapdragons, which we delivered from a rumpled station wagon to wealthy Cape Cod dowagers by the sea who commanded fresh flowers in every room, changed every week. Man, how I loved being dirty.

But we were dabblers in miracles unawares, Sally and I; and even Mrs. Chesbrow, I dare say, could not have known the Promethean fire we held in our hands, this teeming, roiling thing we call dirt. Author William Bryant Logan 'fesses up in *Dirt*'s opening pages, "The truth is that we don't know the first thing about dirt. We don't even know where it comes from. All we can say is that it doesn't come from here. Our own sun is too young and cool to manufacture any element heavier than helium." The Lord would be pleased with the disclaimer, I think, He who through Job thundered, "Where were you when I laid the earth's foundation? Tell me, if you understand."

When I'm in the neighborhood, I sometimes pull my car off the beaten path into the Hatboro cemetery. I see my name etched there on granite, and below, the hyphenated date that quivers like an impatient fill-in-the-blanks. It clears my head and I go on my way, less frenetic than before.

"For dust you are, and to dust you shall return."

Man is eventually a fine talcum powder that can be blown off a bridge and carried on a breeze. Wrap him in a $500 or a $5,000 coffin, and double wrap in cement if you please, but the second law of thermodynamics will have its way; the earth reclaims what is hers and was loaned. Cold bodies, with twigs and matted leaves together, boil themselves down to an organic residue that is the matrix of all life: humus.

Only the commonness and abundance of it keeps us from phoning our friends with excitement over humus. As Mr. Logan explains, "Some of it releases nitrogen and trace elements for the reuse of plants; all of it nourishes the microbes, which decompose it and whose bodies add to its substance . . . unique among biological substances, humus resists the processes of microbial decay, so that it can remain in the soil, sometimes for ten thousand years or more. And we know that this is a good thing, because it can hold mineral nutrients for a plant's use twice as well as the best clays."

There is a painting in my house of a man and his wife bowed reverently over their rakes at evening. What are they praying? Are they thanking the Lord that in autumn "the tide of bases in the soil climbs into the finest pores of plants—the tissues of flowers, leaves, and fruits—whence they fall to the ground?

Within a day, almost half of the fallen tissue has been digested by the microbes and invertebrates growing in the ground. The acidity of the soil recedes, and it prepares for its slow, neutral, winter life, making an equilibrated medium to protect the roots until the spring"?

Hardly likely. Nor even that "an acre of good, natural Iowa soil burns carbon at the rate of 1.6 pounds of soft coal per hour." They are saying instead, "Thank you, Lord, for another day of life, of health in our limbs, of food on our tables, and of a promise that when these mortal husks have fallen, 'He who raised Jesus from the dead will also give life to our mortal bodies.'" The miracle of dirt will not even enter their minds.

# DISCOMFORT ZONE

*When the church bulletin has a "help wanted" notice*

I HAD NO INTENTION of being anything but a warm body from 11 a.m. to 12:30 p.m. in the "4-year-olds" Sunday school class at my church. There was a hole that wanted plugging—a need for "teachers" and "helpers" had been announced mercilessly in the bulletin for weeks, until the steady drumbeat of call to obligation had become an intolerable tug on the conscience. In any case, others had taught my kids in Sunday school, so the logic of it was inescapable. I chose the wallflower position of "helper"—sharpening pencils and clearing Ritz cracker crumbs off tables, I hoped.

The reader must not be too condemning here. I had been badly burned in a valiant attempt to teach fifth- and sixth-graders in a local public school that I'd hitherto perceived to be high in common-grace levels. And even well before that, from a thousand little deaths, the verdict was in that I am singularly unsuited for working with children. I have watched crackerjack teachers in action and have noticed that one salient ingredient in those who've "got it" is a discipline of mind that I will call "presence in the moment," which I have notoriously lacked all my life, being a hopeless Walter Mitty. And I have reluctantly bowed to the conclusion that if one or two kids are intractable it's the kids' problem, but if all 25 are intractable, it's the teacher's problem.

I realize there are two schools of thought about serving in Sunday school. One is that the Creator has endowed us with certain gifts and that we are responsible to use these, and to let others use their own as they have been apportioned; and that everything should work out swimmingly this way: the well-oiled body of Christ with every distinct part humming in its place. But there seemed something suspiciously self-serving about this theology as I tried to recuse myself from the child-care sphere of church life.

The other school of thought, of course (which the elders would have pointed out to me if I had attempted to wheedle out of service invoking the first school of thought), is that one should be willing to step outside one's "comfort zone" and serve wherever there is a need. I settled on that second philosophy, and stepped into the class of Mr. Steiger, for better or for worse.

One must always remember when entering a classroom of children—and especially when this is the start of their third hour in the church building— that they will have a different agenda than the teacher's. The teacher may be thinking how interesting it is that there are nine fruit of the Spirit, or that the tabernacle in Israel was first located in Shiloh, but it is a rare 4-year-old who will immediately share his enthusiasm. And at this late hour you have going against you not only total depravity but the pent-up energies of stallions too long held in the stall. (I am referring also to myself in this last observation.)

By week three the good news was that I started to learn some of the 22 names, and that personalities began to emerge from the faceless blob of preschool humanity. The bad news was that the kids were in control of the class. At Bible-story time they sat in their chairs—when they deigned to sit at all—like Lily Tomlin in her *Laugh-In* shtick, and called my bluffs when I weakly intimated that consequences might be meted out for lack of cooperation. I began to get butterflies in my stomach on Friday afternoons in dread of Sunday mornings.

I needed to do something desperate. I called Becky W., a fellow church member who had half these kids in her class at the nearby Christian school, where, the rumor was, they were pliant and docile as Rubens's cherubs. We met at Barnes and Noble, I with pen and paper, eager to plunder her best games, time-fillers, and strategies; she, with messages about reaching hearts, getting down to eye level, and the subliminal instruction that goes on in the teacher's every choice and gesture, way before you crack the catechism open.

I am learning a lot in Sunday school these days. Last week a girl ran up and hugged me, which warmed the temperature of the room considerably. Also, I bought two puppets at a craft fair, borrowed the pastor's daughter's puppet stand, and discovered the effectiveness of one degree of separation between me and the audience when communicating a Bible story. This doesn't mean I'm signing up for next year, but then again, you never know what God will do.

# Making a ball 'dance'

*The universe doesn't readily divulge
such mysteries as the knuckleball*

THE TAJ MAHAL IS a pretty nice building and the Eurostar ain't no shabby train, but for pure wonder consider the knuckleball. Consider it now as the boys of summer wind down their pursuits: "the strong men are bent, . . . and the doors on the street are shut, . . . and desire fails, . . . and mourners go about the streets, . . . and the dust returns to the earth as it was" (Ecclesiastes 12:3-8). Consider it now as the "curse of the Bambino" clots the air over Boston, the Chicago Cubs are once more uninvited to the Series, and Hoyt Wilhelm (1923-2002), master of the knuckleball (aka "butterfly ball" aka "floater") has passed from the scene in languid August.

"The evil that men do lives after them; the good is oft interred with their bones. So let it be with Caesar" (Mark Antony in Shakespeare's *Julius Caesar*). So let it be with Hoyt, too. And even if his mortal coil goes the way of Ted Williams to immortal refrigeration, could we ever know the secret he carried to that way station to eternity?

My college teacher said that when evolution had got itself a full head of steam, the brain reached a critical mass of complication and one day gave birth to consciousness. The idea seemed puerile to me even then, like a silly child's tale with a giant ellipsis. For matter is matter, and mind is mind, and the twain touch only by mystery. Likewise, no locus will be found, in the dissected folds of Hoyt's gray matter, for the knuckleball "wonder of the world."

Of course God knows the way to it—through and through and in and out. For He planted it there, like some cosmic scavenger hunt, to be discovered by men. That was on the same day that He brought forth Wisdom as the first of His works "when He assigned to the sea its limit, . . . when He marked out the foundations of the earth" (Proverbs 8:29); when He showed the mountain goats how to give birth and taught the hawk to fly and the horse how to leap like the locust (Job 39:1,20,26). The knuckleball was there in Eden, waiting.

I picture a boy, a bored little goatherd in 4,000 B.C. His companion has gouged sheep guts and fashioned a lyre of sorts. The boy, less musically inclined, is pitching rocks. Since that is his only occupation other than corralling the odd stray billy, it is perfected over time: a science, an art. The boy learns spin. He tries spit. He experiments with knuckles. A new thing is born in the universe.

Though maybe not this scenario. For the secret is in the seams, and a rock has no seams. It's the stitches on the leather, as much as the instinct in the hurler, that makes a knuckler what it is, and very few men now in the game have whipped it into submission, most notably Tim Wakefield of the Red Sox. A mere three practitioners are in the Hall of Fame—Phil Niekro, Jesse Haines, Hoyt Wilhelm. The universe does not readily divulge its mysteries.

Little Leaguers will be inspired to apply themselves to their school science lessons where so much is at stake, for the knuckler is a formidable weapon in the pitcher's arsenal, so nearly impossible to hit (and to catch!) that even Angels contact hitter Orlando Palmeiro, who has rarely whiffed all season, was fanned three times by Mr. Wakefield's gravity-defying antics in the Aug. 15 game. (Bobby Murcer said trying to hit a knuckleball was "like eating Jell-O with chopsticks.")

Boys will pore over wind-tunnel measurements. They will ponder that a spherical object pitched in a vacuum speeds unfettered through the void, but that the invisible ether that inflates our lungs and gives lift to 747s also creates delightfully exploitable circumstances in the 60-foot journey from mound to mitt. They will spend hours fixing thumbnail, forefinger, and middle finger, stiffening the wrist, pressing ball to palm with the left hand, perfecting the "push-off" to minimize rotation and maximize a beneficial turbulence. Aerodynamics will take over, the stitches producing the imbalance of forces that just might make a ball "dance."

They will be tempted to add to the Bible, in wonderment, the following tribute to the glory of God: "Three things are too wonderful for me; four I do not understand: the way of an eagle in the sky, the way of a serpent on a rock, the way of a ship on the high seas, and the way of a man with a virgin" (Proverbs 30:18-19).

. . . And the way of the knuckleball shimmering toward home plate.

# IT'S GOOD FOR SOMETHING

---•---

*War is problematic,*
*but earthly peace is not the highest good*

I TOLD MY KIDS that Philip Berrigan of the "Berrigan Brothers" just died, and they thought he was half of a rock group. So we did a little ancient history (the Vietnam War) and I explained that it was also local history, since two Catholic priest anti-war protesters took hammers to warheads at the General Electric Nuclear Missile plant in nearby King of Prussia, Pa., and were tried and convicted in Norristown, our county seat.

The children and I then went a few rounds over war and "what is it good for?"—their view being "absolutely nothing!" and mine being hard to fit into a slogan because I knew I would have to drag the whole Bible into it, which no one was in the mood for on a short drive to get sushi.

I was about to remind my fellow passengers in the car (who outnumbered me three to one) that the Old Testament was pretty much just one long string of

wars interrupted by occasional peace, but they beat
me to it. Their take was that war is an abomination,
and that just as God says He hates divorce (Malachi
2:16), and merely regulates it (Matthew 19:8), he hates
war too. This is a good college try, but not as tidy a
parallel as they would like because God not only
regulates wars, but calls for them now and then.

To be perfectly pugnacious about it, a good case
can be made that one of God's attributes is that of
warrior: "The LORD is a man of war; the LORD is
His name" (Exodus 15:3). Furthermore, while it can
possibly be argued that the little skirmish at the
Red Sea around 1400 B.C. was a case of self-
defense, or a freedom struggle, the series of wars
begun 40 years later in Palestine cannot by any
stretch be so characterized. The Canaanites were
just minding their debauched business (sacrificing
children to Molech and such) when the Lord slated
them for destruction. "You shall save alive nothing
that breathes" (Deuteronomy 20:16).

War is problematic for my thoroughly modern
children (and for every thinking soul). It would
seem to bring into collision two prominent themes
of Scripture: God the warrior (Isaiah 42:13), on the
one hand, and on the other, God the lover (1 John
4:16), the compassionate (2 Corinthians 1:3), the
merciful (2 Samuel 24:14-15), the hater of violence

(Ezekiel 12:19). But, I ask you, my children, would love be love—would it be compassionate, merciful, and a hater of violence—if, say, it let the murderer of your best friend go on his merry way?

Can we then at least establish, considering all the above, that if God is against war, He is not against it categorically? That extenuating circumstances may justify it? "For everything there is a season, and a time for every matter under heaven . . . a time to love, and a time to hate; a time for war, and a time for peace" (Ecclesiastes 3:1,8). The highest good is not earthly peace but heavenly peace. Earthly peace has given us such things as the tower of Babel and Sodom and Gomorrah, after all.

The Lord has a score to settle with the nations of the earth, and it will not come about without violence. It will be as in the days of Joshua, when the heavenly host, the sun, and hailstones all fought on his side (Joshua 5:14; 10:11-13). That first time was a sip of His justice; the second will be the full cup (Revelation).

The "Plowshares 8" was the other name the Berrigan brothers went by, which moniker I'm sure they were happy to pinch from Isaiah 2:4: "and they shall beat their swords into plowshares, and their spears into pruning hooks." This is a wonderful vision to hold in the heart, and will surely come to pass when He returns, and war will cease forever, and the tree of life will spread her boughs for the healing of the nations. But until then, I am afraid, we are still in for a little more of this: "Beat your plowshares into swords, and your pruning hooks into spears" (Joel 3:10).

# An "author's tea"

---

*Sin and its effects don't fit on a 3"x5" card*

BECAUSE LIFE IS SHORT, I drive with tapes. So many sermons, so little time. This particular jaunt was to school for an "author's tea" featuring my favorite author—and her 16 first-grade colleagues. The particular portable pastor en route was preaching about sin (he was against it). "Hate what is evil," quoth Romans 12:9, and I tried to get on board but maybe was just in too good a mood.

Besides, the verse grates, like fingernails across a blackboard. Hate is something terrorists do. Hate—against anything—is increasingly bad form in America (e.g., "hate crime" laws), considered downright hillbilly. If there is a congressman out there who harbors such a flower in the secret garden of his heart, he had better not parade it in public but sublimate the thing with something high-minded, say, indignation. Hate is out; tolerance is in.

At the moment, it was hard to feel anything but gleeful anticipation as I entered Miss Wagner's

Room 10 for an event that had received top billing at our house for two months now, the culmination of a semester of assiduous phonics and "guess-and-go." The perfect dress had been laid out a week ahead, the book's plot kept so secret that the FBI director should blush. My only role was cupcake-bearer.

In the classroom, chairs had been arranged in a circle, where seating was intuited: parent-child, parent-child—like one of many patterning exercises I'd pulled from the homework folder of the afore-mentioned author. Spaces filled in quickly for the 9:15 a.m. reading of the junior authors' original bound works. And I in my seat, biding time, studied the faces of entering parents with their progeny, looking for similarities in the curve of a nose, the turn of a smile, a body type.

That's when I noticed him, the little guy 180 degrees from me, the only gap in the circle that wasn't filling in, though curtain time was now 5 minutes late. Then, finally, 15 and 20 minutes, and we had to begin.

Maybe it was nobody's fault. Could be a single parent situation, and mom or dad just couldn't get off work. Or two parents and neither could be excused, for all their trying. Could be the traffic, or an accident on the way (heaven forbid). Or a sick sibling at home. Or a sudden emergency. Or Mom forgot. Or maybe the darned notice just got lost in the reams of daily communications.

And then again . . .

What is sin, anyway? When I was a child, sin was a no-brainer. You brought them on a 3"x 5" card to the priest at Confession, citing the specific Mosaic commandment violated, with a convincing tally of the number of infractions since the last Absolution: "I stuck my tongue out at my sister . . . 6 times." (More lying was done at Confession than any other time of the month.)

In adulthood, sin became more difficult to wrap my mind around: Sin was the discrete act of commission, but also the proclivity you were born with—to anger, to timidity, or to sloth—that in the right environmental soup will cause one man when he is weary simply to sigh, and the other to reach for a bottle of Dewar's. Sin is the methodically planned bank heist, and sin is a fondness for afternoon naps that leaves the rafters sagging. Sin is "defiant," or sin is "unintentional" (Numbers 15). It is the ooze secreted at Eden that just generally gunks up everything. It explains the World Trade Towers, and it explains a 7-year-old boy alone at an author's tea.

I am not one who thinks little kids' grief is little

grief. I remember. And now, in Room 10, yours truly was feeling hate without even trying (the sermon tape was kicking in). Hate, and anger, and sorrow, and all the sad songs of the world—at no one in particular. Diffused and generalized free-floating protest with nobody to alight on. I was mad because a little boy was sitting across from me, a crayon-colored, hard-bound book on his lap, two skinny, dangling legs that didn't reach the floor, two hands covering his face so that no one could see him. Noiseless tears.

A woman better than I quietly invited him to sit near her and her daughter, and our half of the circle each moved down a chair. The child read his book with dignity—a story, as it happens, about his mother's birthday, and dedicated to her.

I went home afterward to a quiet room and found the place where it is written of a better day to come: "He will wipe away every tear from their eyes. There will be no more . . . pain, for the old order of things has passed away" (Revelation 21:4).

# Snowstorm psychology

*Enjoying one day's respite from war and rumors of war*

THERE'S SNOW AND THEN there's snow. We got the second kind last month—that school-closing, SUV-shaming, every-mother's-child-delighting storm we were deprived of last winter. We were more than fairly compensated: "five oxen for a stolen ox, four sheep for a sheep" (Exodus 22:1).

In an instantaneous mental shift of gears, I chuck the day's work and find shovels. These will be my unsuspected weapons against the encroaching agents of suburban isolation: "Something there is that doesn't love a wall, that wants it down."

I will pluck my way first to the "new" neighbors I forgot to greet with pecan rolls—it's been a year, at least—and hope they have not cleared the steps and sidewalk yet. Should I knock on the door and introduce myself, letting these hibernators, still nameless, know whose handiwork this is? I consider, and then think better of it: The bondsman of the

Lord does not let "the left hand know what the right hand is doing"(Matthew 6:3).

Others have appeared now, a rag-tag army wielding each his homely implement to desecrate the artistry of heaven. I try to take it in before it is too late, the sculptures inviting conjecture that Flora, Fauna, and Merriweather have dusted off their wands from Sleeping Beauty fame and kindled anew their competition: We see unearthly topiary where the shrubs stood yesterday, curvaceous swells and depressions round the trunks of pines, perfect pompadours topping marooned cars, an impossibly tall meringue of snow astride a picket fence, windswept dunes like folds in the train of Queen Esther's Persian wedding gown.

Once again in history, "the earth takes shape like clay under a seal; its features stand out like those of a garment" (Job 38:14).

"Natural revelation" goes a long way with me. The Creator leaves His calling card in the nooks and crannies, which none but anointed eyes may read (Romans 1). My heart momentarily is panged for the impoverishment of those who labor by my side, who have no One to thank—the soul must be slightly sickened when gratitude has no addressee. The circle of delight, for them, is not complete. Joy is occluded at the point of giving birth.

"He was in the world, and the world was made

through Him, yet the world did not know Him. He came to His own, and His own did not receive Him" (John 1:11).

People will be friendlier today, a snowstorm psychology that nobody understands but everyone expects, a 24-hour brotherhood of man that sparks a hundred conversations between folks who have lived doors down from each other for 30 years and never spoken.

My kitten, a smudge in the unrelieved whiteness, mews atop a crest just out of reach, terrified at the loss of terra firma, licking the strange white crystals off one paw and then another. I had tossed her out the door this morning, as usual, and she had gone willingly, unawares. She will not come now though I implore with outstretched arms, for fear of sinking in the dust, which is too powdery for snowman dreams, by dint of 20-degree temperatures. I perform the daring rescue in shin-high boots reinforced inadequately with "tall" kitchen trash bags.

The snowplow has forgotten our street. Through narrow trenches carved like moats before every man's castle, I make my way to the end of this desolate outpost, and on a mischievous impulse walk with impunity down the median line of Keswick Avenue, regressing for an hour to a time when children played kick-the-can in Bowery streets, and man still seemed to stand a chance in the turf wars with Henry Ford's machine.

The baker, the dry cleaner, Ralph's barbershop, are abandoned. I imagine I am one of the hardy few surviving The Big One we learned to fear in Soeur Ange Marie's third grade: We hid under our school desks and pictured something called "fall-out" drizzling on stranded cars, perhaps a white powder not unlike this present draping.

I am brought to remembrance of the riddles God put to Job, among which: "Have you entered the storehouses of the snow, or have you seen the store-houses of the hail, which I have reserved for the time of trouble, for the day of battle and war?" (38:22-23).

In this time of trouble, Lord, we thank Thee for this respite of the present day, the confirmations of Your sovereignty and love.

# THE 'WIDE' WAY

*A widened heart views others with hope and
possibility instead of with a severe, loveless accuracy*

FOR ME EVERYTHING IS biblical. Even Disney's
*Brother Bear*, as pumped with New Age clichés as a
Unitarian Sunday school class, is helpful to my
piety. Each loincloth-clad noble savage, at his coming
of age, is assigned a "totem," a pendant with one
unique word on it ("patience," "love," "bravery," etc.)
to be the focus of a lifetime, the mantra of the
journey, the divining rod of discovery of the secrets
of the universe.

It isn't a bad idea, to my thinking, that rather
than Bible knowledge a mile wide and an inch deep,
we contemplate the possibilities of the man on a
desert island who's salvaged only one scrap of
Scripture from the shipwreck and has to chew on it
the rest of his life. I have a theory that almost any
passage of the Bible is a doorway leading to every
other passage eventually. Just master one and
you've done all.

My "totem," I have lately decided, will be 2 Corinthians 6:13: "widen your hearts." I have never heard it preached on, nor given it much thought myself—which is qualification enough. Beyond that, it would seem at first blush to be more promising than, say, a verse on how to dispose of the offal of a bovine offering (Leviticus 4:11-12).

The desert island will have to be a sort of Gilligan's Island for this to work, a place with at least a few inhabitants to rub up against, since the presenting problem, of course, is other people.

My guess is that Paul appears prickly to many of us. This may be his lack of adeptness in the art of shmoozing. Be that as it may, his letter to a church that's been gossiping along the lines of "his letters sometimes evince a fine turn of phrase, but he isn't much to look at or such hot stuff when you meet him in person" is disarmingly childlike in its vulnerability. Somebody with a heart not "wide open" might dismiss him as either groveling or peevish:

"We have spoken freely to you, Corinthians; our heart is wide open. You are not restricted by us, but you are restricted in your own affections. In return . . . widen your hearts also. . . . Make room in your hearts for us. . . . for I said before that you are in our hearts" (6:11-13; 7:2-3). This is painful to listen to.

It wasn't till I decided to try opening my heart

wide that I began to realize how constricted it is by habit, how narrow an opening I give people—either to get in in the first place, or to stay in. Lack of practice tells in almost every encounter. "She's a bit off, isn't she," I mentally assess in the midst of a conversation. A preacher preaches Christ and I find 10 things wrong with the sermon.

(All the while, of course, my preference is that others would use the "wide open heart" policy toward me.)

Paul's phrase, "widen your hearts," is so loose, so nontechnical, so undefined, so . . . wide open, as to coerce some outlay of cogitation on my part. What it means to "widen your heart" I am evidently free to explore without restriction, since I am so unlikely to go too far with it that, as with other virtues Paul names, "against such things there is no law" (Galatians 5:23).

I discover there are two ways of seeing my brother. There is the "merely human" way (1 Corinthians 3; 4)— a severe, loveless accuracy. A clinical fixation on the wart on his nose. A covering the sun with one finger.

Then there is the "wide" way. It sees possibility; it is full of self-knowledge; it "believes all things, hopes all things" (1 Corinthians 13:7); it regards the other as "a new creation" (2 Corinthians 5:17) and abandons the tired modes of "measuring" and "comparing" (2 Corinthians 10:12). It is the difference between mercy and justice, kindness and shrewdness, remembering one's own reflection in the mirror and forgetting. If I possessed it, then when I met someone who dislikes me (I may only be imagining it), I would say to myself, "Gee, I wonder if he's not feeling well today." Or I would say to myself when the postman is surly, "My, aren't we humans a piece of work? Why, I was surly to a café customer myself just the other day."

So "widen your heart" is my new "totem." I think about it all the time. Now to get it down to one word for my pendant. Maybe "love"?

# OLD-FASHIONED LOVE SONG

*It's best to let sleeping passions
slumber until their right time*

OUT OF THE WHOLE of Plato's *REPUBLIC* that a college professor tried to drum into our heads, I recall only the opening exchange between Socrates and the aging Cephalus on the subject of youth. To the philosopher's query as to whether life is harder toward the end, his geriatric friend replied that though some may say so, for his part he was relieved to have escaped the "mad and furious master" of the more youthful pleasures. This resonated with a 17-year-old who could already see that love was a problem—a force associated with anguish, bondage, obsession.

And yet, to be done with the season of love and to be glad of it? O Cephalus! My soul recoiled at the thought.

Now I am widowed and sobered and closer to Cephalus's portion of the journey than ere I was, and more wont to look for answers in the

Scriptures than among the ancient Greeks. I thought it befitting to come to God's Word and look again to the locus of wisdom on Eros.

What do you do with Scripture's Song of Solomon? It is the uncle in your living room that nobody talks about. He's part of the family so you have to let him in, but he's just so weird—and vaguely threatening. I have yet to hear preaching that goes anywhere near it, except to offer some obligatory concession that sex is a beautiful gift of God. May we hazard the presumption, on the basis of "inerrancy," that we can learn something from this encrypted poem, something "profitable for teaching, for reproof, for correction, and for training in righteousness" (2 Timothy 3:16)?

Our betters tried for centuries, to be sure, and history is littered with their attempts. The old Greek translation, as well as Josephus and Philo, does not allegorize away such sensuality as "hair like a flock of goats," and "browsing among the lilies." Hippolytus and Origen are another matter. These early Christian interpreters, with body-despising hangovers from Platonic dualism, can divine only the divine, seeing nothing under any spreading tree but metaphors of Christ and the Church—and doubtless there exists no small grounding for this in Hosea, Ezekiel 16, and Revelation 19.

I am not sharp with poetry more sophisticated than Robert Frost, but I know a literary device when I see one, and I have wondered for years about the cryptic refrain in verses 2:7, 3:5, and 8:4: "I adjure you, O daughters of Jerusalem, . . . that you not stir up or awaken love until it pleases."

Modern interpreters, eager to establish their enlightened credentials, see in Song only unalloyed tributes to the joy of sex, and the "do not arouse" mantra as a call to let love be spontaneous. Heaven forbid this is the message for our times. Spontaneity in sex is the one commodity of which I should have thought we had enough.

I am grateful for a book by Professor George Schwab of Erskine Seminary, *The Song of Songs' Cautionary Message Concerning Human Love,* for hearing in Song the minor chords as well as the major, the whisper of caution in the valley of God's delights.

It is fun, I suppose, to feel faint like the "Beloved" who sighs in the quicksand of her emotions, "I am sick with love" (2:1-7). There is some kind of pleasure, I suppose, in a frantic search through village streets in wee hours for one's lover (3:1-5; 5:2-8). But it begins to seem, too, that love has its drawbacks.

Falling in love can be debilitating, enfeebling,

and all-consuming. You forget to eat. You cannot work. You certainly wouldn't want to live this way over a prolonged period, as the "songs" of this world would have you do, encouraging serial lapses.

"'My lover is mine and I am his'—covenant language. He is one sweet tree in a forest. She is a flower, all others are brambles. Exclusivity is the hallmark of love when pleased to be aroused" (Schwab).

But love is a sleeping tiger, and Song a solemn warning of its bottled-up danger, a force which if approached unwisely will consume a man and all he has (8:6-7; Proverbs 5; James 1:14-15; Jude 8; Revelation 18:3). Are you ready for these feelings?

I have been young and now I am old, and I adjure you, O children of Jerusalem that you "not awaken love until it pleases." Heed the caution, that you also may enjoy the garden in season. The wise man will take care for his affections and keep them in the bounds of God's design, while the foolhardy will tickle the slumbering Leviathan before its time.

# HOUSE OF MOURNING

*Funerals are opportunities to hear
the best, and worst, of theology*

THANK GOD FOR FUNERALS, the one place left where non-churchgoing America comes touching close to truth. I've been to two this month. You hear the best and the worst of theology at funerals. The best cuts right to the chase, boring down to bedrock theology like a 17th-century Scottish preacher: "The Lord's Supper is coming over the Cairngorms to your town next week; you're either in with Christ or out; make up your mind, laddie," cries the circuit rider. None of this waiting till salvation is on the liturgical calendar before bringing up the subject.

I am today a black speck in a black sea of well-wishers; Cheryl was a much-loved lady, I surmise, though a mere acquaintance to myself, the mother of my son's friend. I did not weep at my husband's funeral but I am weeping here as I peer through heads at two stoic teenage boys I never knew owned suit and tie, boys who think they are grieving but who are not yet grieving as they will. I weep because I know what is ahead for them.

What these around me know I cannot tell. Some, as we wait for the interminable greeter's queue to end, have lapsed into talking about business, vacation plans, and the best manicures in town. This is not offensive to me, as I prefer it to officious sullenness, yet I cannot help drifting to the scene in *Live and Let Die* where a feckless bystander cranes his neck over crowds at a New Orleans–style funeral down Bourbon Street and asks who the corpse is, only to be unceremoniously stashed into the casket himself. "Ask not for whom the bell tolls; it tolls for thee."

A collective spiritual insight almost breaks through, then is submerged again—as if some invisible, malevolent incense inhabiting the belfry would keep us all sleepy and OK with death. I struggle to stay awake, for I am as susceptible as any. "Leave the dead to bury their own dead," says Jesus, and I understand now, since the preacher tells us, "Death is not life cut short; it is one of life's phases." (I jot this down on my program because I cannot make up such pap even if I try.) He proceeds to inform us, with breathtaking confidence, that Cheryl is at this very moment "looking down at us with a tear and a smile" and mouthing sweet words (that he has made up for the occasion).

But I am not here to deconstruct funerals. I start praying for truth, and things start looking up. "Jesus is the Resurrection and the Life," the priest says. And, "Do not fear; only believe," he implores. I want to believe, but I have seen his kind before, and I want dearly to ask him, "Would you be willing to say these same things half an hour from now at the back door? Or at my kitchen table? Or will I find myself betrayed again by your embarrassment?"

I follow through the rest with the sure-footedness of someone inbred from childhood with its smells and ritual, producing a "sign of the cross" on cue from some ancient place within, and forming all the right responses. I make a split-second decision about the doctrine of Transubstantiation, *ex opere operato,* and the appropriateness of partaking of the elements.

As we file out through the vestibule I'm thinking that there is a fine line between celebrating someone's life and a hagiography, a fine and treacherous line between celebrating Cheryl and eclipsing the Lord of the manor. The overall impression must be the thing, I decide: In the afterglow of the funeral, who is glowing most—Christ or the dearly departed? It's all so subtle: Who can pin it down, or call it right or wrong, when many of the words are right but the music is just slightly off?

Still, "It is better to go to the house of mourning

than to the house of feasting" (Ecclesiastes 7:2). A day is coming when it will not be so, when "Thank God for funerals" will be an appalling thing to say. For like the ark of old, these things "shall not come to mind or be remembered or missed" (Jeremiah 3:16). But for now I see this as a strange amalgam of special and general revelation—at its best, when the gospel is sharp and clear, the former; at its worst, still the former. And may the small seed sown in the last two hours not be snatched from the rocky path as soon as the church doors shut.

# PERSONALITY PROFILE

*Schaeffer gave a life-changing
explanation of a personal God*

ONLY ONE THING MATTERED about God in the beginning. I have in decades since been briefed on His other attributes—infinity, sovereignty, holiness, omniscience, righteousness, aseity. But these are all refinements, in a sense, of the only question that was important to us in the '60s— whether god was personal. Every mother's fool had been versed in college in a lower-case and upper-story god who was the "ground of being." Cold comfort.

Like the dragon of Revelation 12, the Enlightenment had crouched at the delivery room door to devour Personality as soon as it was birthed from the Bible. Paul Tillich nibbled at it in the theology school and Freud finished it off in the psychology school. Personality was dead by my generation, collateral damage of science unmoored from Christendom. There was no "you" there, we were coolly told—all dissected and deconstructed into a gaggle of libidinal urges, with nothing at the center. Personality remained only as a chimera, a Hallmark card, the crutch of wimps not "worthy of their beards."

A 1959 *Twilight Zone* episode, "The Lonely," nails the dilemma. A convicted murderer is banished to an uninhabited asteroid for 40 years, serving his sentence alone in the universe—except for the presence of a robot dropped off via supply ship. She looks like a woman, talks like a woman, feels like a woman. And when one day a flying saucer from Earth appears with parole, she cries tears like a woman. After agonizing, the prisoner, over the baffled entreaties of his liberators, elects to live out the rest of his days on the asteroid with his ersatz companion.

An honest man born after Freud must at this point ask himself about the movie: "What is the difference between that robot and my wife, really?" In a less than honest (or consistent) moment, Freud himself, the man who killed love, writes desperately to his fiancée, "When you come to me, little Princess, love me irrationally."

Just then, when Kerouac's *On the Road* seems the only life option, my brother Marc pulls from his knapsack in 1971 a new find, *The God Who Is There*, and before I get past the title I am "disbelieving for joy." The author, Schaeffer something, names the cause of our collective depression before we can name it ourselves. We had been alone in the universe. We had had enough of "god" and were ready for a god who was *there!* Our bodies and minds had ached for it—our experience had fairly demanded it!—but our educations had forbidden it. We had lived close to our presuppositions and far from reality, and the trip was starting to tell.

Brothers, what happened next is hard to explain, but when God became a personal God a few things ensued simultaneously, like the call of a lark as the signal to awaken the whole woodland. It threw open the windows to music. Everything was delicious—Smetana's *Moldau,* Beethoven's 7th, Birchermuesli, the Alps, old Mr. Ruchet bent over his cane, the strength in our limbs, the drip-drip of icicles dissolving into spring from the eaves of our chalets in Huemoz sur Ollon.

A recent trip to the attic lured me from my purpose to a dusty volume I unshelved and, slouching in a corner, thumbed through once again, curious to know if what I'd felt so long ago was the impressionism of youth and nothing more. He speaks my language still. He has one song in all his books—of a Personal God who is there and who is not silent and who makes this place a personal place and gives my life meaning—and I love the way he sings it.

When I walk down the street in Glenside in 2005, I walk differently than if Francis Schaeffer had not lived a continent and a generation away. Because of *The God Who Is There,* I make eye contact with the pedestrian who enters my space, conscious of the presence of another authentic personality created by the Personal God who is the father of us both. I do not see him as Camus's *The Stranger*. For this I make my tribute to Francis A. Schaeffer, not as other tributes I may have made in this column: This one is personal.

# BEGGAR'S MORSEL

———————•———————

*A discerning way to run toward
the homeless instead of away*

I UNDID A DOZEN years of nightly Bible reading
by walking past a beggar with my son in
Philadelphia. Calvin called me on it immediately in
a noisy altercation right there on Market Street:
What about "love thy neighbor"? What about "be
open-handed to the poor"? I stammered some
unconvincing self-defense about how one has to
be wise, how the fellow will probably drink it.
Finally, out of nothing more exalted than shame, I
filched a dollar from my purse and gave it to Calvin
for the figure squatting under a blanket.

The March 22 *Philadelphia Inquirer* had a little
story with photo on an unmarried 29-year-old
defender for the Kixx (our pro indoor soccer team)
who runs toward homeless people instead of away.
I decided to check it out. I looked for the green
jacket on a grassy commons in front of the main
library at 19th and Vine, where roughly 200 milled

about, some waiting in queues for macaroni by the ladle, others having their blood pressure taken by physician's assistants in training from the local Hahneman Hospital.

In another corner I spotted a huddle of humanity like somebody was giving away money. Guess what? Somebody was giving away money. I stood on the periphery watching the green jacket take requests ("Need ID?") and tear off personal checks at a speed that brought to mind a 30-year-old incident in Guadalajara that involved hastily disencumbering myself of a couple of hundred dollars in travelers checks as the price of informal Mexican justice.

"You were easy to spot," I spoke up when he noticed me. "I don't have much of a wardrobe," he replied, waiting for me to state my business. I told him I write for a magazine (partly because I always thought it would be cool to say that) and asked for an interview. He scribbled his phone number and moved on to nobler business. Exiting the premises, I was swept into the Hahneman vortex and got my blood pressure checked: 100 over 60.

Later I asked Adam Bruckner for his story, assuming (correctly, it turns out) that he's one of us—another aimless traveler snatched up, in spite of himself, onto the Kingdom train barreling down the track toward the Apocalypse. He was your average cynic from suburban Milwaukee who at some point started looking at the Bible for real instead of to stump people. "My heart changed from dark to light and I couldn't explain it."

The heart burden for down-and-outers came over months of shuffling from state to state trying out for soccer teams. It's where he learned all the needs—and all the scams, too—and realized that you can enable, and not "enable," by offering checks to the order of Penn DOT (driver's license) and Pennsylvania Vital Statistics (for birth certificates) and not straight cash. "I know the system and who to write checks to and what the requirements are." (You need ID to work at Burger King.)

"Does anyone underwrite you?" I asked, perplexed. "I get a few donations, but much less than I spend. Last year was a very expensive year and I will not be able to continue at that rate. That being said, I know that God will provide a way for it to work. . . . I have been without a car several times and had to take trains and catch rides to serve the meals. (He spends three hours cooking on Mondays at Helping Hand Rescue Mission, 6th and Green Streets.) One time my car wasn't starting regularly, but I knew that it would or the food wouldn't get there. I find myself repeating, 'All things work together for the good of those who love God and are called according to His purpose' (Romans 8:28)."

"Any advice for the church in helping the needy?" I inquired. Mr. Bruckner: "No money, no rides, no promises. I think you need to approach these men with open arms of love . . . but with an awareness that there is some darkness . . . and to proceed with caution. . . . There will always be scammers; many of the stories are not true and the more questions you ask, and asking for references and details, will show who has good intentions. Either way, you can't fake being hungry and cold."

# You were available

*A message to adulterous women
who think their cases are special*

WHERE PEOPLE GO WRONG is that they think they're unique. I'm convinced of it. No one ever fell into adultery who didn't think her illicit attraction for the paramour was a special case, the burden of unbearable destiny, a saga soaring high above—and not governed by—the laws that apply to other mortals. No one ever loved like this, she thinks. No one ever found herself yoked with a like agony, or suffered such outrageous fortune.

I am speaking to women. Men are a different species entirely, a fact that becomes clear after marriage. Those creatures from "Venus" who do not accept the fact can be found in counseling offices, trying till doomsday to change the leopard's spots.

I say nothing but what Genesis predicted. Men are not relationship-driven in quite the same way as their mammaried counterparts. Call me a stereotype perpetrator, but your quarrel is with

Andrée Seu

Scripture. Here we are apprised of a cleavage in psychology as fundamental as it is universally underestimated. To the woman after the Fall the Lord talks relationship: "Your desire shall be for your husband" (Genesis 3:16). (The Hebrew word for "desire" is the same as that used later to describe sin's "desire" for Cain.) To the man the Lord talks about hassles at work (verses 17-19). Relationship is already not his primary orientation; he's into seeds and John Deere and tinkering in the garage.

(My 24-year-old daughter judges men by the look in their eyes. My 22-year-old son has a checklist of measurable attributes. Enough said.)

Every woman contemplating an affair should take a field trip to a men's locker room. In that inner anti-sanctum she would learn that affairs are not the same for him as for her. He is not the mystic she is. He is not wont, between furtive passionate episodes, to congregate with friends over latté, there to sigh and dream and mewl. You will find him in undistracted concentration on the company's quarterly financial report, studying the Eagles stats, and perfecting his golf swing. Knowledge by women of this fact alone could obviate more incidents of adultery than a hundred fire-and-brimstone sermons.

That little e-mail flirtation you've got going? The

one where you feel like Edith Piaf? There are 10 million just like it crisscrossing the ether over America every day. How do you feel now?

Self-flattery is the culprit. "Why shouldn't you—even glorious you!—be as grand as God?" the unctuous one insinuated to Eve, and it has been our Achilles heel ever since. Would it help you to see, o woman in adultery, just how interchangeable you are for him? You were available; that's all.

There is One who is unique—His accolades tumble out of the Bible: "the Holy One of Israel" (Isaiah 1:4); "O Most High" (Psalm 9:2); "the Lord our Righteousness" (Jeremiah 23:6); "I Am Who I Am" (Exodus 3:14). And so Eve's misunderstanding is also the chief misunderstanding of all men of all times, the heresy of the confusion of Creator and creature.

Antidote: The "Our Father" once a day: "Thy kingdom come." "Thy will be done." Christ's template prayer doesn't get around to your own personal needs till the second half, by which time the petitions seem shrunk to the size of a supply requisition list for the better arming of ground troops for service.

Know that men have affairs for reasons, not because you are their long sought mystical "other half." Hello! These Romeos are not looking for more relationship, they're looking to escape relationship—

the gritty, time-consuming work of living with their own wives "in an understanding way" (1 Peter 3:7). You, fun-time lover, are a feast at Le Bec Fin that he doesn't have to clean up after.

Is there no encouragement? How can the sister find happiness in marriage and not roam to other cisterns? One way only: Keep your relationship with God as the primary one in the triangle. (For singles, a startling discovery: You can love a man without owning him; prayer partnership is real relationship.) Herein is your joy and ability to love your mate. And a promise is attached: "To the one who conquers I will give . . . a white stone, with a new name written on that stone that no one knows except the one who receives it" (Revelation 2:17). Unrepeatable. Outstanding. Unique.

# PUPPY LOVE

—————— ◆ ——————

*Learning to love God, man,*
*and beast—in the right order*

I DIDN'T WANT A dog, so this year we got a greyhound. There's a story behind that and my three older kids tell it differently, but I repudiate the charge that I always cave in to the fourth child.

In any case, I found myself at the greyhound adoption center in northeast Philadelphia, submitting to an interview (by a formidable woman aptly surnamed Gunner) to ascertain my worthiness for this commitment that I was sternly assured would claim 12 years of my life. I was ready for her, having endured a like abasement for the privilege of our cat, the protégé of a militant feline rescuer whose handwritten road sign we responded to four years ago. She it was who first disabused me of the idea that one just "gets a pet."

Was I aware that my dog would require a biannual sonic teeth cleaning ($120), and between visits a good brushing with a DentiVent Fingerbrush and toothpaste? That on specific dates I was to administer the "Heartguard" and start the Doxycycline (for tick-borne diseases)? The correct proportion for meals is 2/3 dry food and 1/3 canned, plus two tablespoons water to moisten. I am to watch for self-esteem and separation anxiety (leave her an hour every day to obviate the latter). Would I mark on my calendar the two-week and six-week progress reports? My dog has been microchipped; send in $12.50 with registration fee to AKC Companion Animal Recovery.

All the world's a stage, and I played my part well in the kennel office, I thought, stifling the impulse to exclaim, on seeing the medal-bejeweled collar, "Cool, this is the first dog I've ever had with tags!" I looked convincingly horrified when Gunner snarled, "Would you believe we had one client who kept the crate all the way on the other side of the house in the laundry area, away from the family room!" I didn't flinch when she lapsed into dog-training language in addressing me—as when I proudly announced that I had driven a spike in the backyard to tether my greyhound for fresh air, and she said, "No!" "Bad!"

It was hairy on the home front too. Aimée wanted to name the dog "Artemis" and I drew the line there, citing conscience objections and Acts 19. Aimée thought that ridiculous, but I told her I will not open the front door every day and call out the name of an ancient Ephesian goddess in the hearing of my neighbors for whom I'm praying knowledge of the true God. I won this one; the dog's name is Spider.

Every love has a dark side. Mothering can become smothering. Eros can become exclusive of the rest of the world. Friendship can degenerate into a snobby mutual admiration society. Sometimes it's easier for a foreigner to see our imbalances, as when my brother-in-law (fresh from Seoul where they eat dogs) dropped his jaw the day he spied a postcard on my table from a local veterinarian and addressed with treacly sentimentality to my beagle, Cookie. Giving in to a perverse urge to unsettle him further, I told him about dog psychiatrists in New York.

That's all fun and games, but Dr. Jekyll becomes Mr. Hyde if unchecked by the restraining power of a higher affection. The FBI's deputy assistant director for counterterrorism, John Lewis, told a Senate committee in May that animal- and environmental-rights activists are this country's top domestic threat of "violent crimes and terrorist actions."

Do we love our dogs too much? I am inclined to extrapolate an answer from C.S. Lewis's musing in *The Four Loves* on whether we may love people too much: "It is probably impossible to love any human being simply 'too much.' We may love him too much *in proportion* to our love for God; but it is the smallness of our love for God, not the greatness of our love for the man, that constitutes the inordinacy."

"Whoever is righteous has regard for the life of his beast" (Proverbs 12:10). In the next 12 years (if Gunner is right), the Seus will be working out the bugs of learning to love God, man, and beast in their proper order and proportion.

# REMARKABLE PROVIDENCES

---

*How a flu bug launched a head-injury camp*

CHARLOTTE LEFT GEORGIA TO care for her dying father in Texas. She ended up coordinator of the brain-injury program at Baylor Institute for Rehabilitation, where she and the chaplain thought it might be fun to organize an overnight camp for former patients. Then she married Mike in 1991, and in 1993 they retired to Red River, N.M.

Or so they thought.

A flu nixed plans to visit family in Texas at Christmas. Meanwhile, former patient Michael B., getting nowhere on the slopes, dropped in for a chat and inquired about a possible head-injury camp in Red River. With no forethought, Charlotte said, "Oh, it will be in August." That was eight months away.

First she needed lodging on flat terrain and scrounged up 20 cabins seven miles from town. Two days later the preacher of Faith Mountain

Fellowship church braved a snowstorm to pay a pastoral call. Before leaving he committed his church as camp headquarters and meal venue.

It was time to phone Baylor Rehab about possible co-sponsorship with the church. She found favor beyond expectation: Her former associates promised six paid staff members.

Transportation. No national rental companies had wheelchair vans, but Charlotte talked to a lady in Boston who knew a lady in Albuquerque (the nearest airport to Red River) who had two. Southwest Airlines offered discounts for groups traveling on a Sunday.

As the question of start-up costs dawned, out of the blue came $300 "to help offset a few administration needs." J.S., ex-wife of a former Baylor patient, got wind of the camp and offered a nonprofit foundation, her own residential program that was no longer operational. A simple name change was all the lawyer needed to make the transfer. A year's worth of work done in a phone call.

Next up, insurance. No companies had the right type. Then one night Charlotte substituted as ski hostess for a friend, which involved meeting a tour bus at 2 a.m. The bus was late. To stave off sleep, Charlotte idly perused a file from J.F. It contained a travel insurance policy from an outfit in Ft. Worth. The following day Charlotte's group had coverage.

Charlotte had her heart set on T-shirts. Companies wanted $1,500—too much. The day she gave up that quest the phone rang with a donation of $1,500. Charlie D. from Amarillo volunteered to cook. Pede S. from Baylor apologized for not being able to come to camp and sent four huge boxes of craft projects. Red River townsfolk rallied round the camp vision when one of their own, 10-year-old Nathan L., suffered brain injury in a skiing accident.

Campers need scholarships. Charlotte and Mike inserted donation requests in their Christmas cards. A steady stream of small checks came in, simultaneous with the stream of seekers. Neither was totaled for months. In May they did the math: $1,275 in needs, $1,275 in scholarships. The mayor and his wife, asked to present the souvenirs, decided to fund them: staurolite rocks, shaped like a cross and found in the Sangre de Christo mountains.

Who do you call to provide punch and cookies when you've already tapped out the town? Margo S., owner of a local bar, read about the camp in the church newsletter. She rang and asked whether Charlotte could use refreshments. OK, cups with "Bull of the Woods Saloon" imprinted on them.

Charlotte was mentioning to God that she needed two more people to lead fishing expeditions. Just then two people walked by her cabin, an unusual sight where most folks ride horseback. Charlotte ran down the driveway and invited them inside. Owners of the cabin down the road, turns out they just love to fish.

Two days before camp they were two cars short. The Mahurins from Oklahoma dropped in to see how they could help. They had two cars. Still one vehicle short for the three-hour airport drive to Albuquerque. A nurse from Moriarty, east of Albuquerque, called to discuss first-aid kits. "I have to pass by the airport; is there anyone I can pick up?"

Much is left out—how death seeded life; detours turned to shortcuts; rain turned to rainbows; and Mountain High, a five-day camp in Red River for young adults with brain injury, was born.

# STRIKE UP THE LYRE

*Old and new can meet in
today's songs, hymns, and spiritual singing*

JOHN M. FRAME'S *Contemporary Worship Music* has
a dedication "To the New Life Churches, who swim
against the current of Reformed opinion for the
sake of the Reformed gospel." I am embarrassed to
say that coming across that tribute was my first
inkling of being engaged in a quasi-political act on
Sunday mornings. One simply gets used to things
the way they are, whether hymnody or psalmody or
"Indelible Grace." (What would the anti-CWM folks
say about rollicking, roof-raising rhythms in the
African-American church down the road, I wonder.)

It must not be assumed that because I am a
"boomer" the guitar is naturally more congenial to
my soul than the pipe organ. In my childhood town
of French Canadian transplants, I elbowed into the
choir a year earlier than was the rule, and we lisped
only in Latin ("*Tantum ergo sacramentum . . .*") and
French ("*Il est né, le divin enfant . . .*"), following some

unquestioned conviction that these pleased God more than the vernacular, which any old commoner could understand.

So I didn't take easily to the raising of hands and eruption of spontaneous smiles during the serious business of praise, and even penned a letter of complaint to the elders (which I rather hope has been incinerated), calling for a return to what was good enough for a couple of centuries of Christians. The upstart music, I protested, seemed the product of two guys with four chords in a garage, and the lyricist needed a course in "Verbal Advantage."

That was a bum rap. As author David Foster Wallace says, "For me, the heavier the stuff gets, the littler the words need to get. The most important stuff is reflected in the vocabulary of a fifth-grader." So *"Vive la difference!"* We mix it up in my church—one "How Majestic Is Your Name" (Michael W. Smith) for every "Crown Him with Many Crowns" (Matthew Bridges and Godfrey Thring). And many Psalms as well. Some brothers prefer the old standards, and others the newfangled, so we compromise in deference to one another and to our weekly visitors ("all things to all men").

Now I have my favorites from columns A, B, and C. But that's all beside the point, of course, if

God objects to being worshipped with drums and electric bass. Yet we take our orders from Scripture alone (*sola Scriptura*), which says nothing about 18th-century music being holier than 21st-century, or "thou" being better than "you," or Hammond organs more spiritual than Yamaha guitars. The unflattering truth is that I am a recovering musical snob—some latter-day Michal despising David from her latticed window, scruples barely concealing the devil in her heart (2 Samuel 6:16).

I know a church that sings the Trinity Hymnal's "None Other Lamb" but won't touch "In Christ Alone" because word got around it was written by one of those modern pop worship guys. You tell me how Rossetti and Wiseman's 19th-century song is holier than Stuart Townend's 2002 inspiration.

Turns out there are all kinds of reasons why one likes or hates a song that have less to do with theology than with where you were when you first heard it. I figure the critics of contemporary Christian music are as susceptible to historical nostalgia as I am to high-school nostalgia. It's amazing how much better even our junior-high worship team, with its sledge-hammer rhythms, sounds now that I've changed my attitude from Salon.com critic to worshipper in spirit and truth.

Why not embrace all kinds of reverent and God-honoring song as a way of loving the brethren? As we enlarge our tents to make place for organ, fiddle, lyre, horn, and drum, we acknowledge that God's heart in this age is an evangelizing heart.

Modernity and reverence. No necessary contradiction. "The Little Drummer Boy" sings: "I play my drum for Him" (i.e., it is only a crude and humble thing that I am able to bring). He also sings, "I play my best for Him" (i.e., I don't bring Him sloppiness but only my utmost for His Highest).

And brethren, sometimes on a Sunday morning when the rafters are swaying, I think I see David in linen ephod, thronged by all Israel, with trumpets and shouts, and dancing before the Lord with all his might (2 Samuel 6:14-15).

# ANDREE'S APHORISMS

*The longer I live, the truer the Bible gets—and other things I've learned*

YOUR FRIEND'S CASUAL JOKE about her husband is a deep well. Probe and you will find pain. | *Whole lifetimes are wasted worrying about the opinions of people who aren't even on the right wavelength.* | A lot of what I thought was my personality was just sin. | *People laugh at your unwholesome talk at the moment but think less of you afterwards.* | I started out wanting to be my children's savior, and ended up pleading for forgiveness.

❧

Marry a man who loves God more than he loves you. | *Grand witnessing is spoiled by not returning the Tupperware.* | Make a phone call, keep a friend. Neglect a phone call, lose a friend. | *Even awful family outings become fond memories over time.* | Living in regret of the past, or fear of the future, are two ways of not living at all. | *Better to let your child make an imperfect bed than to have a perfect bed that you make yourself.*

♍

An inferiority complex is a desire to be better than other people. | *The more you see how wretched and needy you are, the less the question "How much should I pray?" is an issue for serious debate.* | I complained, "God hasn't answered my prayer." That's because I was not looking for help in my weakness but for the removal of my weakness to the praise of my own glory. | *Sit on a sensitive letter for three days before sending it.* | A phone call to say, "I'm thinking of you," yields benefits all out of proportion to the time investment. | *The best teaching moments are never at convenient times.* | When I have no intention of obeying a Bible command, I say it's not meant to be taken literally.

♍

Be known as faithful. If you say, "Let's do lunch," do lunch. | *While inside an idolatry you love your idolatry. When you are set free you see what bondage it was.* | There is no need to boast about good deeds. They have a way of getting found out even if you hide them. | *Now and then skip the dishes and run out to the park. In 20 years your kid will remember the park and you will not remember the dishes.* | Thinking a lot is not the same as praying a lot. | *An idol forfeits your life. You look back and say you never lived.* | The hard part is when you're still holding back something from God. Give it over and be surprised at how much easier it is.

God is the better chess player. Just obey. | *You're one prayerless day away from being capable of any sin.* | Talent is good, but faithfulness is better. | *My kids have a foggy recollection of things I tried to teach them, and total recall of my phone conversations they overheard from the next room.* | My kids have a rough recollection of my Christian propaganda but reproduce my attitudes with a cloned precision. | *Tell your child what delights you about him. He doesn't know unless you tell him.* | Your child is never angry for no reason.

Break a fear-of-man problem by aggressively loving people. | *Practice one command of God earnestly*

*rather than a hundred sloppily.* | The fool thinks that tomorrow or next Tuesday his problems will be over. | *Be open-handed with money for building others up. Life is short and the Lord always supplies more.* | If you wait for better times to "Rejoice in the Lord" you will never do it. | *Praising and thanking God all day long are the only cure I've found for depression.* | There are a finite number of days. Serve the Lord while it is Today. | *Drop the dust rag and look at your child when he's telling you a story.*

God will not be trifled with; He is Lord. | *Let your words be few.* | Pray on the spot for the person who comes to mind. It's either pray or sin. | *I don't regret not cleaning more. I regret walking past the bedroom door of a girl who fell silent after sixth grade, and not seeking out a boy who sat alone and cried at a family vacation in the Poconos. Forgive me, Hae Linn. Forgive me, Jae.* | If you're not dead yet there is still time to repent. | *The longer I live the truer the Bible gets.*

# GET REAL

*We all have stories, but who
is the main character?*

OLD FARMER BROWN IN the back pew has drifted off as soundly as Eutychus toward the end of a sermon, when suddenly comes the first whiff from the pulpit that a story is abrewin'—an anecdote, a shard of autobiography, or even a joke (crass cousin and truncated form of story). The farmer is roused awake.

To say that people like stories is like saying Jacques Cousteau liked a day at the beach. We imagine we enjoy stories as we enjoy a Snickers bar now and then, but there is something profound afoot. Who ever considers what atavistic forces draw us into a story's grip? What soul-imprinting makes us mesmerized by the trajectory of beginnings-middles-ends, and deeply satisfied by the structure of chaos proceeding to resolution?

The rookie writer learns that story is a good wedge into essay, the warm-up act for a more serious agenda. He thinks of story as a gimmick, a device, a prelude to his logical exposition of a subject, which is presumably the grownup part.

But what about our movies, novels, and the serialized escapades of co-workers' lives that we relish around the water cooler? Are we not awash in story all the time?

The politician is a storyteller, no slouch to Garrison Keillor. He doesn't talk to his constituents about war or taxes in the abstract. He tells a story (perhaps a tall tale) of how it all began, of how we got ourselves into this predicament—because of the opposition party. He casts a vision, the glorious sequel of how life will turn out if only we elect him.

My marriage is done now. And if you asked, I have a story, which my mind rehearses regularly, of how my marriage went and what it was all about. It has antagonists and protagonists, and I have honed it, over time, to a perfect internal consistency. It feels truer with many repeatings.

Story is how we learn theology. The way to appreciate how the Bible is written is to imagine how it is *not* written. Not a systematics textbook, not a manual for how to get saved. It is stories: trouble in Paradise discovered (Genesis), peace in Paradise restored (Revelation).

You can look at Jesus' penchant for storytelling two different ways. You can say He was unfortunately born into a culture of storytellers and so He did the best He could with primitive tools. Or you can say God knew what He was doing when He picked ancient Palestine for the setting of His great salvation, so that generations hence of cultural snobs, who thought they had outgrown stories "in this day and age," would be forced, in spite of themselves, to suckle on the marrow of parables, extracting wave after wave of riches.

My friend the Christian counselor said everybody has a story, a sort of personal saga. It is sometimes a fictional story. It is always a selective story. The counselee is the star. Satan told Eve she had the wrong story, and he magnanimously supplied a different one—with her in the center. The goal of good counseling is to help the counselee fit his story into the Bible's story. I myself have taken to praying the "Lord's Prayer" daily to realign my story—which had gotten out of focus over the previous few hours.

There is nothing more tragic than to walk around all your life in the wrong story—thinking yourself a knight-errant and mistaking windmills for giants, skinny stable horses for noble Rosinante, and unexceptional peasant girls for Dulcinea.

C.S. Lewis writes, "I can imagine no man who will look with more horror on the End than a conscientious revolutionary who has, in a sense sincerely, been justifying cruelties and injustices inflicted upon millions of his contemporaries by the benefits which he hopes to confer on future generations: generations who, as one terrible moment now reveals to him, were never going to exist. . . . The future Utopia had never been anything but a fantasy."

Reminding yourself of the real story is good for what ails you. If you've gotten too high and mighty, it reminds you that you are "dust." If you're feeling like dust, it reminds you of your glorious destiny.

"Awake, O sleeper" (Ephesians 5:14), and get with the real story.

# ALL YOUR MIND

———————•———————

*It's for a good reason that the
Christian life is not a to-do list*

JOSEPH FOUND HIS BETROTHED to be with child—and not by him. "Being a just man and unwilling to put her to shame, [he] resolved to divorce her quietly" rather than throw the book at her (Matthew 1:19). Small footnote in Scripture; big leap in this reader's understanding. Here was a thinker, a grappler, who wrestled within the parameters of righteousness and found one way more excellent than another.

Father Abraham, there was another thinker. He "considered his own body, which was as good as dead." Then he thought about the promise of God "that he should become the father of many nations." Then he thought about God's track record for keeping His word, and Abraham emerged from that mental exercise deciding to trust in God (Romans 4).

Mary "pondered" (Luke 2:19), and Daniel "sought

to understand" (Daniel 8:15), and the Psalmist cried, "Search me" (Psalm 139:23). None of them thought it unscriptural to be analytical, or a usurpation of the Holy Spirit's role to engage their faculty of reason. The Lord was in the process.

If the Pharisees had known what it meant to love the Lord with "all your mind" (Mark 12:30) and not to reduce righteousness to rote rules, they might have understood why mercy is better than sacrifice (Matthew 12:7), and why money donated to the Temple does not absolve you of obligation to your parents (Matthew 15:1-9), and why people hanging around Jesus don't feel like fasting (Mark 2:18-22).

I have often wished the Christian life were a to-do list dispensed daily from on high, eliminating guesswork:

❑ *Today, call your mother*
❑ *Increase your tithe by $20*
❑ *Send Calvin to Philmont Christian Academy*
❑ *Read this book, not that one*
❑ *Move to Winnsboro, Texas*
❑ *Plastics!*

I would gladly comply with that kind of piety. But I think the Christian life is by faith in order that it be by engagement of "all your mind" (Romans 14:5b).

How would you like it if your husband gave

you his body and paycheck but showed no interest in getting to know you? God wants your mind more than your tithe. Likewise, the second great commandment is a mental workout, too, say Allender and Longman in *Bold Love*. Who is my neighbor? How does a mile in his shoes feel? How can I love him for his own good?

They say we use just a fraction of our minds. I do. Something is bugging me—dull, like a pebble in the shoe—and I just live with it, carrying free-floating angst all day. Why not set my mind to name it, and locate the "root" of that bothersome "fruit" (Luke 6:43-45)? The unjust steward in Luke 16:1-8 didn't blubber but brainstormed. "Crying is all right in its way while it lasts. But you have to stop sooner or later, and then you still have to decide what to do" (C.S. Lewis, *The Silver Chair*).

Self-diagnostic questions: Why am I miserable? What desire of mine is being frustrated? What is it I fear? (Here you will face some ugly truths.) Follow the process through and you are brought to a decision point. What was amorphous before is now a fully conscious raft of options.

I don't know what the inside of your head looks like, but mine looks like *Guernica*. You don't realize how out of control your thought life is until the day you try to rein it in. Redeemer, redeem every part of me, "take every thought captive" (2 Corinthians 10:5)!

Some things I've decided in my mind you would probably call legalistic. There are foods I don't do because they lead me to weight gain, and weight gain to depression. Depression, in turn, hinders my race. Ergo, donuts are sin for me, but not for you. (It's just between me and God.)

My friend Barbara's hip starts aching and she knows it's time for a visit to the chiropractor, and he does this thing with her ankle and it puts her whole body back in alignment. What's good for hips and cars is good for minds. I take regular inventory: "OK," I say to myself: "What is it I said I believed about Jesus?" "Do I have good cause to believe it?" "Shall I continue to follow Christ or not?"

Jesus once put a demoniac "in his right mind" (Mark 5:15). I thought about that and figured He can do it again.

# THE OLDER WOMAN

On being a fruitful tree in "late autumn"

THE OLDER WOMAN" IS the target of a twin cultural broadside: the stereotyped battle-ax of a whole industry of mother-in-law greeting cards, and the taboo seductress. Mammy Yokum of *L'il Abner* or Mrs. Robinson of *The Graduate*.

The Bible takes a different view. Older women are to "train the young women" (Titus 2:4). There is an expectation of progress in the Christian life, not just a treading of water till Christ returns: "And we . . . beholding the glory of the Lord, are being transformed into the same image from one degree of glory to another" (2 Corinthians 3:18). "Grow in the grace and knowledge of our Lord" (2 Peter 3:18).

Someday, in spite of all your tummy tucks, liposuction, organic food offensives, and fitness workouts, someone will walk up to you and say, as a woman said to me last Sunday: "Would you be willing to mentor me?" And then you will realize that the jig is up: You are officially an "older woman." When that happens, I hope you will have better things to say than the stuttering disclaimers I use to recuse myself. You will not want to be one of those "fruitless trees in late autumn" (Jude 12).

For in that late autumn, you are meant to bloom still. The orchard of God wants ancient sequoias whose "leaves remain green, and [are] not anxious in the year of the drought, for [they do] not cease to bear fruit" (Jeremiah 17:8; Psalm 92:14). Where is the permission to dye your hair blue and grab a free senior-citizen bus pass to the Showboat Casino in Atlantic City?

Jesus came upon a tree that, from a distance, had great promise, its tussled head of greenery bespeaking nourishment. On closer view, it had no figs. "And He said to it, 'May no one ever eat fruit from you again'" (Mark 11:12-14). The vineyard owner came and found no grapes three years straight, and in exasperation said to the vinedresser: "Cut it down. Why should it use up the ground?" (Luke 13:7). These tales are no more about trees than "you shall not muzzle an ox" (1 Corinthians 9:9) is about oxen.

There is something jarring about a hoary pate where no wisdom is found. "Like a gold ring in a pig's snout" (Proverbs 11:22), like a fool living in luxury, or a slave ruling over princes (Proverbs 19:10), it is disturbingly unnatural, an upset of the created order. During my college-day summers I worked in a nursing home, and it was a great disappointment—like coming to an oasis and finding it a mirage.

In a land where the sons of Ponce de Leon still seek the fountain of eternal adolescence, where pearls are marked down for quick sale while baubles are inflated, who will embrace the last of the great rolling spheres, where Anna's prayers saw no surcease, and Jacob worshipped over his staff?

A child asks in *Children's Letters to God*, "Dear God, Instead of letting people die and having to make new ones why don't you just keep the ones you got now? Jane." I venture an answer to Jane: God's big idea in constituting the world with babies, teens, middle-agers, and seniors is that as we navigate the different rings, we glorify God in the manner fitting to that peculiar stage: "The glory of young men is their strength, but the splendor of old men is their gray hair" (Proverbs 20:29).

The plan is that as the woman's first beauty wanes, a ripening comes that is the second beauty. It is by this that men may still love their wives, even as the bridal dowry of physical allure is exchanged, over time, for the better dowry of an inner glow.

Twentysomethings, you are headed my way. The message of Proverbs is that destinations are reached one step at a time. Maturity does not come stapled to your AARP membership. Some day, only turn around, and suddenly a younger woman will tap you on the shoulder and say, "Will you mentor me?" Be ready. You will not want to wonder if the husbandman would say about you, "Cut it down. Why should it use up the ground?"

# Next Tuesday

*Replacing "Lord, help me trust in You"*
*with "Lord, I trust in You"*

STARTING NEXT TUESDAY I'M going to praise the Lord like gangbusters. That's when my meeting in Harrisburg is over and I can exhale. How wonderful it will be then, the white-knuckling behind me and the joy in Christ before me. For now, I need to worry.

I'm going to rejoice in the Lord, I really am, but I cannot rejoice today. Today, all sleep-deprived, my goal is just to muddle through till bedtime when I'll catch a solid eight and be in shape to "reign in life" tomorrow.

Woe is me! The same old sin has snared my soul again. I have repented copiously, but how could I, vile sinner that I am, come to His gates with joyful praise without a proper pause (of several days) to beat my breast and stay away and suffer for my wretchedness? Psalm 51 pleads, "blot out my transgressions" and "restore to me the joy of Your salvation," but surely David doesn't mean today. Must keep respectable delay of time betwixt the two.

I said to Jesus, "Help me trust in Your unfailing love." And then I sank again into morbidity, to hunker down until such time as He saw fit to answer me. No rush, I thought. He is the Lord. What can I do until He acts?

A friend objected to my piety. Not "Lord, help me to trust in You" (quoth he) but "Lord, I trust in You! Yea, by Your grace I trust in You!" There's something psychologically different here, my chastened soul took note: The first prayer has a pious sound but never gets around to business, letting me postpone the joy it seeks a month or two, the meanwhile dithering in unbelief while waiting for divinity to bring me 'round robotically. The second prayer enlists the mind and soul and will, no more defaulting into foolish thoughts of Tuesday next.

Paul commands, "Rejoice!" (Philippians 3:1). David says, "Rejoice!" (Psalm 32:11). But that will have to wait a week or two 'cause now I'm in a stew. There's something I want badly and I must be anxious till it's mine. A major life decision has me tied in knots until it's made. And Satan has a laundry list of reasons why I should not sing (Zechariah 3:1). So pray excuse me from the banquet of His joy: "I have bought a field, and I must go out and see it. . . . I have bought five yoke of oxen, and I go to examine them. . . . I have married a wife, and therefore I cannot come" (Luke 14).

No. This nonsense stops today. Not "I'll rejoice someday," but "I'm rejoicing now." Not "I will trust someday," but "I am trusting now." I have decided that William J. Reynolds' hymn, "I Have Decided to Follow Jesus," is not Arminianism but decisiveness. Once a day or 50 times a day, as needed, I will fight off fear with praise.

"Life is a series of problems. Either you are in one now, you're just coming out of one, or you're getting ready to go into another one" (Rick Warren, author of *The Purpose Driven Life*). Next Tuesday is a vain imagining. And you will never just coast into joy but you must take it by the horns.

For joy must be intentional or it is no match for anxiety. God shows the way out of heaviness and into joy: You best put on "the oil of gladness instead of mourning, the garment of praise instead of a faint spirit" (Isaiah 61:3). The hour is late, next Tuesday never comes, and faith in God is now or naught. Time to stop this stumbling in defeat and live in joy that's worthy of the gospel.

The dog bites and the bee stings and you're feeling sad. But blest are those who praise God in the midst of it, who praise Him when their heart is broken. "As they go through the Valley of Baca they make it a place of springs" (Psalm 84), not vainly waiting till such time as Baca falls into the sea—which verily it will one day, but not, perhaps, next Tuesday.

Put on your dancing shoes, baby!

# LEFT OUT

*Street preacher says the Good News*
*is only good for some "tribes"*

SATAN KEEPS A LOW profile in the 'burbs where I
live. Lets money, malls, and vague malaise do all the
work. I don't think he's having any fun here, subsist-
ing rather than fine dining on souls hardly conscious
enough spiritually to be capable of interesting sins. (In
*The Screwtape Letters,* C.S. Lewis speaks of the devils'
disappointment with Graft sauce that's insipid, or
with "the lukewarm Casserole of Adulterers . . . who
had blundered or trickled into the wrong beds, in
automatic response to sexy advertisements, . . . or
even because they had nothing else to do.")

In the city Satan is not so much a couch potato. I
go there now and then to be reminded there's a war—
as on Sunday, March 26, to Philadelphia's Harrowgate
Park a few blocks north of infamous Kensington and
Allegheny, where the fifth "Rocky" movie was partly
shot, and people more often are shot.

It was the third day of a three-day Harrowgate

tent revival meeting, and I was bound for worship there when sidetracked by the sights and sounds of street preaching with heart. A man on a box with an amp was bellowing the name of Jesus, and I pulled over by a busted hydrant and got out of the car (locking the door).

While the spokesman continued to speak, I sidled up to one of his companions with the big idea that they could come to Harrowgate and join our love fest.

He asked, "What are they preaching?"

I said, "Jesus."

He asked, "What about Jesus?"

I said, "Jesus saves."

He asked, "Saves who?" (I was starting to be uncomfortable with the grilling.)

I said, "Anyone who repents and believes in Him."

He said, "Wrong. He only came to save the 12 tribes of Israel." He rattled them off: African Americans, Caribbeans, Haitians, Puerto Ricans, Cubans, Dominicans, Guatemalans and Panamanians, Seminole Nations, Native Nations, Argentinians, Mexicans, Colombians, Uruguayans, Chileans, Brazilians.

I asked, "What about white people?"

He countered, "Are you white?" (To be sure of no diluted Hispanic blood, I presume). I said yes.

He said, "You aren't part of the 12 tribes."

I asked point-blank, "Are you saying I'm damned because I'm white?" He answered in the affirmative.

I said, "That's not what the Bible says."

He was holding a worn and color-coded KJV. "Want me to show you?" I said yes. He turned to Matthew 10:5-6: "These twelve Jesus sent out and commanded them, saying, 'Do not go into the way of the Gentiles, and do not enter a city of the Samaritans. But go rather to the lost sheep of the house of Israel.'"

"Are you a Gentile?" he asked. "Yeah, so are you," I said (not quick enough for a better answer from Romans 15:10-12, and not believing at this point that it would make any difference).

"What color was Jesus?" he unsheathed the next sword. "Not black," I said (and now I knew we were going to quibble about shades). He flipped to Revelation 1:15: "His feet were like fine brass, as if refined in a furnace." "What color is brass?" he pressed his case, "especially if it's been put in a furnace?" I admitted it would be dark. He clinched the deal with something about Esau and Jacob and Song of Solomon 1:5: "I am dark, but lovely."

I said, "Let me show you something." (I made a move for his Bible but he wouldn't let me touch it.) I said, "The Great Commission," and he was ready for me. "All the nations" means all places the 12 tribes were scattered and must be ferreted out.

"John 3:16," I said. Blank response from across the chasm. So I summarized, "The world. Anyone who believes."

He countered, "Doesn't mean every last one in the world."

I said, "Tell me, what did God make white people for?"

He said, "For destruction."

I said (feeling a little frightened), "How do you think that makes me feel? Are you OK with that?"

"I'm OK with what the Bible says," he said.

I said, "I don't know whether to pray for you or curse you."

He said, "We can't be cursed."

I said, "That's not the Jesus I know."

He said, "You have no Jesus."

Says him. Even Satan knows that's a lie. And trembles, in the great city of Philadelphia.

# BE SOMEBODY

———— ◆ ————

*Find affirmation in Christ or spend a lifetime
in terror of standing outside the "local ring"*

I LOOK AT WOMEN. It's a bad habit and I have to
stop. I'm a woman myself, and this is not a lust thing,
not in the common sense of the word. I cast surrepti-
tious glances at my gender passing on the street to see
where I fit in the hierarchy of being. I derive assurance
from homeliness and terror from beauty. I grade on a
curve. There, I'm as shallow as that.

When you don't have an internal sense of Self,
you need an external—and a constant supply of it.
You're condemned to roam the earth a parasite. The
restless spirits of Matthew 12 go through waterless
places and have no peace until they find a host.
They do not exist apart from this.

If you tell me I am something, I am something.
But you'd better say it every day, or at least once a
week, because I've become a junkie for your praise,
and my kingdom is in constant danger of over-
throw. Your affirmation feeds my Self.

This is not different from what goes on in hell. The junior demon Wormwood, recipient of formally affectionate but vaguely disturbing correspondence, finally asks point blank if his Uncle loves him. "Love you?" comes the reply. "Why, yes. As dainty a morsel as I ever grew fat on." Screwtape's final communique, after the mission has gone badly, and the velvet glove is shed, is signed, "Your increasingly and ravenously affectionate uncle."

We are all in need of a Self, of being somebody with respect to an outside source of approval. It is not as if there are people who need to be affirmed and other people who don't. It's just a matter of which reference you elect to heed. No one is ultimate enough in himself to be his own final integration point.

In 1944 C.S. Lewis gave the Memorial Lecture at the University of London's King's College. Of all the charges he might have given the eager young scholars, he warned against desiring to be in "the inner ring." "I believe that in all men's lives at certain periods, and in many men's lives at all periods . . . , one of the most dominant elements is the desire to be inside the local ring and the terror of being left outside." Lewis adds, "Unless you take measures to prevent it, this desire is going to be one of the chief motives of your life. . . . Any other kind of life, if you lead it, will be the result of conscious and continuous effort."

Or, failing your "conscious and continuous effort," the Lord, in His mercy, will send a storm into your life. Now when your lover leaves you, and you have a strong sense of your value in Christ, it hurts a lot. When your lover leaves you and you have a shaky sense of your value in Christ, you suffer identity destruction.

Jesus met a woman at the well who had had five husbands. I would guess she had Self issues. I would say she was a hollow in search of filling. Jesus wanted to fill her. He said, "If you knew the gift of God, and who it is that is saying to you, 'Give me a drink,' you would have asked Him, and He would have given you living water" (John 4:10).

Perhaps all lusts are corruptions of good desires. Before "sin, the flesh, and the devil" got a hold of us in Eden, we desired (and we had) sweet intimacy with the Lord—and because of that, with each other. His love, and the assurance of it, were the wellspring from which to bathe our neighbors in nurturing, the hub of a solid soul from which spokes of ministry and not manipulation emanated.

Intimacy is not a secondary agenda of the Incarnation and Passion of Christ. The salvation these wrought were a salvation into the sweet lovemaking of the eternal Trinity. Being some-body, being affirmed, delighted in, held in close embrace, are where reality began and where it all goes to.

Acceptance is tendered: "I will give him a white stone, with a new name written on the stone that no one knows except the one who receives it" (Revelation 2:17). My soul, find yourself in Jesus and be free.

# GREAT EXPECTATIONS

*Blessed are those who wait*
*for the One who comes on a cloud*

JEREMIAH 45, SHORTEST CHAPTER in the book, is a little aside from the Lord to Baruch. My Bible commentary calls it a "word of encouragement." I see it as a trip to the woodshed. I take it personally.

It is the worst of times, 605 B.C. The ship of state called Judah now lists and heels with buffeting winds from both north and south. Centuries of trifling with the covenant now capsize into a slow-motion death spiral of which the book of Lamentations is the dirge. Assyria takes a bite, Egypt will have its turn, and Babylon waits in the wings for the spoils. All that remains is, as it were, two mangled legs or a piece of an ear, retrieved by the shepherd from the lion's mouth (Amos 3:12).

Judah is now a revolving door of kings and desperate shifting allegiances, her sister Israel having buckled years earlier under Tiglath-Pileser's rapacious war machine. Josiah is finished off by Pharaoh

Necho at Megiddo. His son Jehoahaz is forthwith replaced by a puppet, Jehoiakim. But then Necho is famously routed at Carchemish, with Egypt never to rise again to its former height. Jehoiakim vacillates, cowing now before Babylon, now again before Egypt.

In the swirl of insanity, prophets at court multiply like sarcoma, all, to a man, urging patriotism and victory, and a league with Egypt against Nebuchadnezzar. All condemn Jeremiah and Baruch as traitors. Undaunted, Jeremiah continues speaking, Baruch continues writing. They urge an unpopular message: It's no use resisting Babylon, my countrymen, for this is of the Lord, and the purpose of it so set that "even if you should defeat the whole army of Chaldeans who are fighting against you, and there remained of them only wounded men, every man in his tent, they would rise up and burn this city with fire" (Jeremiah 37:10).

Baruch is the scribe of Jeremiah the prophet, the loneliest man in the country. And more than a scribe, a friend. For what scribe is so identified with his dictations that the king has him arrested as he burns up the scroll? And what mere amanuensis, in the final siege, stands with his master as, in a last incomprehensible gesture, Jeremiah buys his relative's field in Anathoth (for there will be a future), even as the sound of the Babylonian horses' hoofs thunder in the distance?

But wait. Does Baruch, that man of noble birth, who could have amounted to something in this world, who gave up everything to cast his lot with the only true prophet, harbor in his secret thoughts the same unspoken heresy as I? Has he been thinking all along that after such and such a quantity of misfortune, one is entitled—yea, one is overdue—for blessings and reward? Baruch brings his complaint to the Lord for redress.

Hark, the Lord now answers: "Thus says the Lord, the God of Israel, to you, O Baruch: You said, 'Woe is me! For the Lord has added sorrow to my pain. I am weary with my groaning, and I find no rest.' . . . Thus says the Lord: Behold, what I have built I am breaking down, and what I have planted I am plucking up—that is, the whole land. And do you seek great things for yourself? Seek them not, for behold, I am bringing disaster upon all flesh, declares the Lord. But I will give you your life as a prize of war in all places to which you may go" (Jeremiah 45:2-5).

What, does the Almighty have pain? Does He weep because what He has built He is breaking down, and what He has planted He is plucking up? Does He grieve like a man "over the ruin of Joseph"

(Amos 6:6)? Over the modern-day ruin in Darfur, Sudan, where the UN has cut food rations to starving refugees? And was I seeking things for myself? Had I great expectations of wretched happiness, and a niche in the American dream?

These are the days of Baruch—the towers are on fire, battlements teeter, the self-lit torches fail. But as for me, I have been spared with my life. And blessed are those who wait for the Lord, who comes on the clouds with reward for His overcoming ones, someday. But not yet. Not yet.

# PROVIDENTIAL WEDDING

*Heidi and John got married,*
*with some just-in-time help*

HEIDI GOT MARRIED ON Saturday, June 10, and that's a long story. But the only part I can get into here is the wedding. Which, by the way, was still up in the air on Monday, June 5, when she and I sat in the Abington Hospital outpatient clinic kicking around a few spiritual issues Satan was delighted to gunk the works with.

Meanwhile, unknown to yours truly, busy bees were erecting the scaffolding of a nuptial celebration piece by improbable piece. You would have to know Heidi to understand. If I had wed in this country it would have been the same, but that was Korea, 1980, and the day was taken out of my hands, including which wedding dress and an impressive multi-tiered cake they wheeled into the sanctuary, photographed, and I never saw or heard of again.

By the way, Heidi asked me to make her wedding

cake, which I agreed to, but only because it was Heidi, and because (as I am trying to impress on you) my friend is as unpretentious as Moses. I was thereby off the hook for other assignments, except maid of honor, which neither Heidi nor I knew anything about.

Janice, a neighbor and third-tier friend, was not even known to me, but someone thought to ask her help with phone calls. This was perhaps the first divinely inspired idea of the preparation. The calls were necessary because the invitations hadn't gotten out till late, which is because they were buried in the back yard temporarily. (Never mind.) Janice has gifts Heidi and I only dream of; to call them organizational and creative would be to demystify the Pyramids. She told me, "I like making something out of nothing." She came to the right place; there was no budget.

Georgina drew up rough guidelines for the potluck wedding reception: green salads, fruit salads, pasta dishes, chicken dishes, bread. No desserts please; there will be cake. Janice, who had prayed, "OK, Lord, bring some good ideas here," had seen a Sam's Club circular and was struck by an ad featuring kids running on a lawn, and in the background many white cakes on pedestals. A cheap way to create a big visual effect, thought Janice, and 10 people were commissioned. She told me later, "The Lord has a storehouse of unasked for prayers just waiting to be claimed."

Our church building used to be a restaurant with ballroom so it was free and not hard to restore to old glory. Sheri donated lots of crinoline from recent family weddings. A little girl named Megan wanted to drape the entryway and was given carte blanche. Swagged material running the long table softened the look. Gini had 20 glass bowls from her own daughter's affair and Janice imagined centerpieces. She opened the crisper of her fridge and brought out green apples and limes. Pale pink roses from a willing neighbor's yard completed the effect.

Paper plates would be understandable, but John (the groom) went to the New Life Thrift Store and they had just received 200 beautiful dinner plates the day before, which they loaned gratis. Thursday night they were short 120 forks but Gwyn, the yard sale queen, happened to be there setting up and calmly said she had that many in her house. Marie donated kitchen commando gifts. Kristen provided busboys and girls from her youth group.

Janice had been eyeing a Korean dogwood in the neighborhood, asking the Lord not to let the white snow-like blossoms fade till after the 10th. She knocked on a stranger's door and asked for cuttings.

The young woman who answered, baby in arms, said she would be "honored."

Becca breezed in Friday night, picked up the icing bag, and did freestyle vines and tiny lavender blossoms on a formerly drab wedding cake. I have failed to tell you the tenth of it—the ceremony itself that surpassed any I have seen for simplicity and meaning.

For reasons beyond the scope of this essay, John and Heidi had to postpone the honeymoon a week. They had planned a meandering route to Florida. Turns out the delay was all for the best; it rained on the East Coast those following days. The new husband and wife are headed out this morning as I write, and the forecast calls for fair weather ahead.

# SLOUCHING TOWARD
# THE COMFORT ZONE

———————◆———————

*Do our churches want to be Acts normal
or American normal?*

EVEN THE NAME OF the church is a little suspicious: "Spirit and Truth." I think it's the "Spirit" part. I was at a Labor Day picnic last year sitting next to a woman who teaches at the elementary school associated with that Philadelphia congregation, and during our conversation she mentioned the Holy Spirit three times. In the old days I would have expressed a need to get up for more potato salad.

Susan Baker is a member of "Spirit and Truth" and looks to be normal, judging from her demeanor at the seminary café where I make tuna cranberry wraps and she is adjunct faculty in practical theology. I thought she might speak to me during these languid summer days. The first thing I noticed is she keeps her office door open. Might not mean anything.

Susan is just a little older than I, so I was curious as to what someone of my generation was doing while I was wasting privilege. Just out of Wheaton College, she and her husband moved into the bowels of Chicago and ran a youth center supported out of their own pockets, doing tutoring, sports, and Sunday school. I asked if she married Randy and moved to the city because they shared the same vision. She said no, she moved to the city because she liked Randy, and Randy moved to the city.

They had gotten a taste for that kind of thing when still single undergrads through Wheaton's "Inner City Christian Action" program, helping a pastor on the South side who converted a factory into a roller-skating rink in the projects. This, incidentally, proves what I have also found, that action precedes love. The only way to get to like doing God's work (which no one naturally likes) is to throw yourself into it. I say this for your encouragement.

The only problem with Randy and Susan's youth group thing was the lack of a good ecclesiology in terms of a bigger church. They would lose the kids in the end. So they started hauling them in their 15-passenger van to the church of a man named Manuel Ortiz. But Manny was called to my fair city and Susan's husband decided to take classes at Westminster, so the Spirit was moving them to Philadelphia. (There goes that word again.) "Spirit and Truth" church grew out of their Bible studies and eventually came under the Christian Reformed Church umbrella, Rev. Manuel Ortiz, pastor.

"Spirit and Truth" seems to be all about church planting. Church planting is church splits that leave greater mass after the operation than before, like a zygote rather than a bowl of ice cream between two brats. Three of their nine ordained elders do full-time community internship. Two of the church plants have just purchased buildings in the last six months. It occurs to me that church planting as a mindset rather than an exotic specialty is closer to the book of Acts than what I normally see around.

I asked Susan why "Spirit and Truth" has so many ordained elders, and she said, "Because we know we're not keeping them." Then I popped the touchy question: Don't you get nervous about the income loss from that constant spawning of churches? She said when the Germantown church left, "Spirit and Truth" lost $40,000—but recouped it in one year by a new influx. Also, mysterious monetary gifts tend to turn up.

This is not to endorse irresponsibility. Susan is the church treasurer, and she doesn't do irresponsible. One of her roles is teaching good bookkeeping to church planters, and how to have good financial statements in case they ever need to go to the bank for a loan.

"Having a kingdom-centered approach rather than a church-centered approach" helps too, explained Susan. "By that mentality we can send out our best leaders."

I asked why this Acts normal isn't American church normal. She said, "Society tends to infiltrate the church better than the church infiltrates society." Slouching toward comfortableness stifles church growth. "If all you're dealing with is transfer growth, then you're just moving people around."

How do you keep yourself from that sinister slouch? I wondered. "I'm not immune to that. I have to be involved in things. If I were not involved in the exciting work we're doing, I would be complacent."

I don't think the Spirit will let that happen.

# THE SOWER SOWS THE SEED

*We await the first fruits of a bumper crop*

RONNIE AND I PUT 10 names in a paper bag and I drew in this order: Daniel, Jae, Leah, Hae Linn, Aimée, David Douglas, David Christian, Calvin, Matthew, Brandon Lee. These are our combined progeny, plus two he wants to cover. We targeted one per week, fasting Sunday sundown to Monday sundown, for 10 weeks beginning April 25, 2005.

He doesn't pray like I'm used to. It threw me off when he would say, "Lord, thank you for saving Daniel." But he claims Mark 11:24 and can't be talked out of it: "Whatever you ask in prayer, believe that you have received it, and it will be yours."

It's late summer of 2006 and we haven't crossed any names off yet, haven't heard the angels' band that strikes up when one soul comes home. There have been interesting developments, though. Jae (my son) landed himself in prison in February of this year. Ronnie and I instantly saw this as something positive.

Still, the days are long. We train our eyes on the horizon and look for Elijah's fist-sized cloud presaging rain. Sometimes I get discouraged.

"How long, O Lord?" (Psalm 13:1).

What do we know about the kingdom? It is like gardening, we are told. Sally and I did Mrs. Chesbro's farm from seed to station wagon tailgate in the summer of '75. We traced a shallow furrow with inverted hoe, tucked zinnia seeds to bed at measured intervals, and covered. We stretched a string from end to end and staked to mark the place. Each morning we would come and check—no sign of life.

One morning you're not sure. You seem to see a fissure running up the aisle like ant earthquakes. Next morning, peeking closely, you can spy the tops of tiny green heads, bent low as if preparing to unfurl themselves, to break out from death clothes. Improbably skinny necks donning hats of earth more than their weight elongate every morn, one hand and then another sprout from who knows where. By July Sally and I had to part our way like jungle lionesses through the leafy boughs festooned with pinks and yellows that we cut long-stemmed for Mrs. Chesbro to make ready for the doyennes of Cape Cod.

"See how the farmer waits for the precious fruit of

the earth" (James 5:7). The garden teaches patience.

The garden teaches mystery. Mrs. Chesbro's feckless farmhand "sleeps and rises night and day, and the seed sprouts and grows; he knows not how. The earth produces by itself" (Mark 4:27-28).

On walks with Spider I pray dragnet prayers, taking in my kids and all their friends. Jessica, my daughter Hae Linn's bosom buddy from adolescent days, I have lifted up to the Lord for a decade, with alternating rote and fervent prayer. About five years ago she suddenly was one of us, and has remained. Was it by prayer? Was it some comment long ago that germinated in the dark? Why she and not another? "He knows not how; the earth produces by itself."

It was but one. And I did not appreciate the sign in it. But Jesus, when they brought Him Greeks, inconsequential trickle in the festal throng (John: 12:20-24), was not so blind to fail to see the thing for what it was: the first fruits of a bumper crop. With distant and prophetic gaze He spoke of seed and mystery: "The hour has come for the Son of Man to be glorified. Truly, truly, I say to you, unless a grain of wheat falls into the earth and dies, it remains alone."

July of 2006. Jesse, Hae Linn's best high-school friend, is in town and says she must see me. A few

Andrée Seu

Novembers ago, Jesse jumped from a bridge; by all rights she should have died. We prayed and she survived. I've said to the Lord many times since then, "Would You save her from the first death just to let her taste the second?" Now here is Jesse in my kitchen sharing her encounter with Christ. I disbelieve for joy until I'm sure.

Meanwhile, the list of 10 remains. I look for ant earthquakes—no sign of life. But movement on the edges gives me trust in mystery.

"Here is a call for the endurance and faith of the saints" (Revelation 13:10).

# A NOTE ABOUT THE AUTHOR

ANDRÉE BEGAN WRITING EIGHTEEN years ago after an aspiring writer moved in next door. On the occasion of her daughter's shedding a baby tooth, her neighbor dropped a poem in her mailbox. Andrée cried on the spot at the sheer beauty of it. Encouraged, her young neighbor started writing more and depositing poems, then essays, then short stories in the mailbox after dark. This "box" tradition continued for a few years and became Andrée's personal school of writing. Beth Kephart went on to be a semifinalist for the National Book Award.

Andrée Seu lives and writes from Philadelphia and is a senior writer for *WORLD Magazine*.

# A NOTE ABOUT THE PUBLISHER

FOR MORE THAN 20 YEARS, *WORLD Magazine* has established itself as the premier weekly newsmagazine written from a Christian worldview. Published weekly except for four double issues, *WORLD Magazine* reaches an average of 135,000 paid subscribers. Among general weekly newsmagazines, *WORLD Magazine* ranks in the top five behind *TIME*, *Newsweek*, *U.S. News & World Report*, and *THE WEEK Magazine*. *WORLD Magazine* regularly features Andrée Seu's essays.

Read Andrée Seu's latest insights in *WORLD Magazine*. To subscribe, write: *WORLD Magazine*, PO Box 20002, Asheville, NC 28802-9883 or call (800) 951-6397. You may also find *WORLD Magazine* online at www.worldmag.com. Be sure to mention the following promotional code when you write or call: WL66AND2.